“*The Un*[illegible]
practical, Bib[illegible]
are relevant to all who seek to live life well. Thank you, Richard Battle, for sharing blessings that have come from your brokenness.”

—Anne Graham Lotz
Speaker & Author of over 20 books

“Richard’s book is for all people, regardless of where you are on life’s journey. It was written as a letter to his son, but the topics, applications, and backup scriptures in each chapter will give any reader valuable lessons for a life well lived. Read this book and then share it with others.”

—Reagan Lambert
Former Director Austin/Central Texas Fellowship of Christian Athletes

“Raising children with integrity, strong character and resilient mental fortitude has never been more needed than in today’s confused and exposed culture. *The Unopened Present* will equip you to parent with confidence and inspire you to build up your family using key precepts and principles that are easily applied and discussed with all ages. The perfect homeschool resource or graduation gift to encourage youth to step forward with influence.”

—Cathy Endebrock
Radio and Podcast Host, “LoveTalk” on The Bridge Austin, Today’s Central Texas Christian Talk, Executive Director, Let’s Pray Today Ministries, Author, “My Voice, His Heart: Experiencing Prayer in God’s Will”

"Richard Battle and I have shared many common bonds and conversations over the last 40 years as if we were face to face trying to share for everyone to hear and act on the many lessons learned from life's journey and our mutual mentors. One of them, former Texas Attorney General John Ben Shepperd, perhaps the best and most patriotic Texas orator of the 20th century, always said, "don't wait until your 21 to be a good citizen…friend… or leader…just get off the sideline now…stir 'em up and get involved.

Richard's book, *The Unopened Present,* offers meaningful thoughts about living life and becoming a responsible and valued person in this very special and free society with which we have been entrusted. The supportive stories and scriptures are powerful, positive, and profound lessons for each of us to share with friends, family, and future leaders of all walks of life that will compel you to want to continue those gifts, through the freedom and democracy of America's founding documents and the 43 messages from Richard to his son, John. In particular, share #32 – Nothing is Free – pay your dues and positively touch others to reap the rewards of life. #35 – Strive for excellence in all things. #39 - Revere the past – it is the wisdom of the ages; #43 – Make friends with as many people as possible. These relationships are the most important thing in life, next to your relationship with God and your family. Then, offer this book to every parent, child, leader, and citizen volunteer with a servant's heart that you know so this *Unopened Present* continues its intended message for generations!"

—Sam J. Chase

Founder & Chairman Emeritus,
John Ben Shepperd Public Leaders Forum/Institute

"*The Unopened Present* is a book that has been long overdue. The Author has compiled years of advice and teachings that are timeless. He uses scripture to support his words. Every family, teacher, student and adult should read this book to give guidance to our lives. "

—Joe Stewart
Past President, Texas Realtors Association

"In Richard Battle's book, *The Unopened Present*, he shares a beautiful message based on a letter he wrote for his young son John who is now in heaven. Throughout the book, he showers us with many powerful life lessons. My favorite 3 lessons are: Lesson #12 - Keep Your Word, Lesson #27 – If You Want to Receive Loyalty, You Must First Be Loyal to Others and finally, Lesson #40 – There are Two Types of People, Those Who Look For Ways to Make Things Happen and Those Who Look For Reasons Why Things Can't Happen - They Both Achieve What They See. I also love how the author challenges us to discern how each lesson applies to us personally. I highly recommend this beautiful book to anyone who wants to be inspired to live their best life."

—Megan Tull
Best-selling Author of "The Passion Belief Method-Own Your Value and Earn Your Worth in Business"

"Richard Battle wrote a letter to his then six-month-old son in 1997 that is the basis for this book. The purpose of the letter was to teach his son, John, lessons in life in case Richard was not around to teach the lessons himself. Unfortunately, John passed away three months later. The letter was, thus, an unopened present. In this book, Richard expands on the original list of 43 points. If we all internalize and live by these rules for living, we will be much happier and will have more success in our lives. If we also share and live by these rules, our children and friends will all benefit. Therefore, the *Unopened Present* is a gift that keeps on giving."

—James Shelton

"Richard Battle's words fall on the heart with wisdom and love. His books feel less like a self-help tome and more like a kind word from a dear friend."

—Rick Mantooth
Broadcast Executive,Community Activist, Speaker, Foster Communications, San Angelo, Texas

"This book has everything a parent needs: solid and honest life lessons to teach our children. Richard Battle not only writes eloquently with wise words of experience, but he also brings emotion, depth, and faith to the forefront of each lesson taught. *The Unopened Present* tugs on the heartstrings yet fills your heart with motivation. It brings the ultimate honor to his late son. With all of his written wisdom that every parent needs to hear, the focus on love shines through it all."

—Bucleigh Newton Kernodle
Award-winning author

The Unopened Present

Richard V. Battle

Headline Books
Terra Alta, WV

The Unopened Present

by Richard V. Battle

To order additional copies of this book or for book publishing information, or to contact the author:

Headline Books
P.O. Box 52
Terra Alta, WV 26764

headlinebooks.com
mybook@headlinebooks.com

www.richardbattle.com

ISBN 13: 9781958914168

Library of Congress Control Number: 2023936560

PRINTED IN THE UNITED STATES OF AMERICA

For John William "The Big Guy" Battle
June 10, 1997 – March 8, 1998

His flame is but a memory,
while his warmth still comforts others.

Table of Contents

Preface

As I humorously relate to anyone curious, my high school English teachers would be astonished if I read a book, much less wrote one.

I never dreamed of writing one book or achieving ten with this volume.

I'll never consider myself an author in the same light as the great novelists and historians. I desire to communicate via the written word as if you and I were conversing.

Whenever you discover my work, I hope you feel like I'm writing every word to and for you, like we're in the room together.

Almost thirty years after the publication of *The Volunteer Handbook: How to Organize and Manage a Successful Organization*, I discovered my life's true purpose.

My mission in all my books, speeches, videos, advisory efforts, and other communication methods is to put forth Positive messages helping people win every day!

My life experiences seem far-ranging compared to my peers, including tremendous successes, setbacks, and challenges. Sharing the lessons, I learned in the hope others may benefit is my great hope.

For example, in *Unwelcome Opportunity: Overcoming Life's Greatest Challenges*, I shared the lessons learned from experiencing a divorce, two heart procedures, and a cancer diagnosis in one ten-month period.

My other passion is lifelong learning, especially history, and what we can glean from our forebearers to make our lives more successful and enjoyable.

I share success stories, quotes, and historical examples of people and events to inspire readers to pursue their lifelong dreams without fear or trepidation. Nearly everyone we can emulate persisted and overcame multiple setbacks in doing so. Their experiences are ours to learn from if we're wise enough to take advantage of them.

Whether you're reading my last book first or the first book last, I hope you'll unearth at least one life-changing idea. As Ralph Waldo Emerson wisely said, "The mind, once stretched by a new idea, never returns to its original dimensions."

May it be your experience and your future path be ever fruitful.

Acknowledgments

Once again, others' knowingly or unknowingly contributed to this book, which enhanced it immensely for the readers' benefit.

Between anticipating John's birth, surviving his loss, and finding a positive path forward, so many people positively influenced my life.

I can't thank John and Elizabeth's mother, Laura, enough for her unconditional and unlimited love and devotion to them.

My daughter Elizabeth is the first and primary beneficiary of my efforts to help people win every day, and I appreciate her love and support.

Buddy and Ginny Jones's wise words at my darkest moment were instrumental in restoring my hope for the future.

Thank you, Wayne T. Franke, for the initial idea to take the original letter to John and add context to the forty-three lessons benefitting others and adding to John's impact on the world.

I'm continually grateful to Logan Cummings, my friend, mentor, and former pastor, whose selfless gift of advice, counsel, and encouragement is priceless to any accomplishments I may achieve.

Thank you to Burke Allen, Shaili Priya, and the Allen Media Strategies team, who represent me professionally but have also become great friends and cheerleaders of my mission for their advice and counsel.

I'm thankful to Doug Wagner for interviewing me on WMT radio, which resulted in the humbling experience described in the chapter, *A Touch from Heaven and Extension of Impact.*

I sincerely appreciate Cathy Teets and the team at Headline Books for their faith in me and this project. Their expertise and contributions were invaluable.

Thank you, Alane Pearce, for your invaluable guidance and editing prowess, for helping me to communicate my message better.

Cover Photo Story

From our earliest memories, receiving a gift-wrapped package causes our heartbeat to accelerate with impatient anticipation.

The beautiful wrapping and gold bow indicate something valuable and magnify the mystery.

What life-changing object is inside? Holding the package with two hands emphasizes careful handling is essential to avoid damaging our gift.

Gifts or presents are given for all occasions, and in many different ways, at various times, from God and people. Some are physical, but the best ones we can't touch.

The question we face is, do we receive them, or are we too busy focused elsewhere?

If we live daily aware of the present time, we can observe and benefit from each offering for our advancement and the service of others.

My son, John, was struck down before he could open the present in the letter I wrote for him. It is here for you and yours to open today and every day.

Like many others, my imperfection and distractions resulted in me missing presents offered for my improvement. Based on my recently renewed awareness, I value each day's present and eagerly look for unexpected gifts that reveal His love.

About This Book

Little did I know where a letter I decided to write my infant son in December of 1997 would lead.

My son, John, was born when I was forty-five years old. I was concerned about living long enough to teach him the important things in life. It was essential to me that he benefit from the practices I had learned without making the mistakes I had made.

When he was six months old, I wrote the letter and filed it in case something happened to me. At that time, I had written one book, which was one more than I had ever dreamed of writing.

Unfortunately, we lost John three months later, before I could teach him these vital principles. His loss redirected my present and all my future present times.

In the following months, healing through reading, journaling, work, and the support of family and friends enabled me to begin caring about the future.

My experiences led me to write *Surviving Grief by God's Grace* in 2002. I included the letter to John in that book, hoping it would benefit anyone reading the book and John's story. I rediscovered the letter while working on *Navigating Life's Journey: Common Sense in Uncommon Times* in 2020 and republished it in that volume.

Similar to a previous book, the inspiration for *The Unopened Present* surfaced and reordered my priorities. Working at the mid-point of another project, I had mixed feelings about changing course; only the paramount importance of this subject eased my discomfort. Hopefully, I'll finish the other project in the future.

This volume expands on the forty-three lessons in my letter to John, adding context and depth to the original teachings. I've added a Scripture verse to each message because of my faith, the plan I had to teach John about God and Christ, and the indispensable Grace I was given to survive and recover from his passing.

I never realized the opportunity to expand on the letter's principles and teach them to John.

The title comes from the unopened present of the letter and the unrealized present days of his life.

Every precept within the letter I extend to you with the prayer that you may find something here to benefit you and your family.

My hope, as expressed elsewhere, is that you will open this present, and it will impact all your future days as they evolve into the present, and you will influence many generations to come.

I believe its message is as pertinent in today's environment as the day I wrote it.

The Letter

"Every day's a perfect gift of time for us to use. Hours waiting to be filled in any way we choose. Each morning brings a quiet hope that rises with the sun. Each evening brings the sweet content that comes with work well done."

—Anonymous

The Dear John Message that Will Lift Every Heart

December 17, 1997

My dearest John-

The following are things I hope to teach you early in life to make you happy, more successful, and richer in spirit. If I pass away before I'm able to personally teach you these things, I truly hope you will take them to heart. I love you very much and I wish you the best for you. I want you to fly the highest, achieve your dreams, and positively impact others' lives. All the while, I hope you will also experience the least amount of unhappiness.

I love you,
Dad

1. God exists. Have faith, pray, and listen.
2. Love and care for your mother. You will be the man of the house. She unconditionally loves you and deserves your love, respect, and attention.
3. Learn early, learn often, and never stop learning. It will determine the level of your success.
4. Remember: You learn more from your mistakes than your successes.
5. ALWAYS have a positive attitude.

6. Don't speak ill of others.
7. Don't listen to negativism. It is a cancer that will deter you from success.
8. SMILE. Say please and thank you.
9. Be sincere.
10. Be on time!
11. Be humble.
12. Keep your word.
13. Be proactive.
14. You will make mistakes. Don't be afraid. It's not how many times you get knocked down in life that counts, but how many times you get back up.
15. "Can't" never did anything. This is from your Papaw Battle.
16. There is ALWAYS an alternative choice.
17. You don't have to know everything, but you do have to know enough to keep from being taken advantage of. Another gem from your Papaw Battle.
18. You are no better and no worse than anyone else.
19. Be VERY grateful for what you have. It doesn't take long to find someone worse off than you are.
20. Have a sense of humor. Things are never as bad as they may appear. A sense of humor will lighten most situations.
21. Anyone can do the things they like. Those who do the things they must do, but don't want to will have greater success than the majority.
22. The "easy way out" is usually only easy in the short run.
23. Think before you act.
24. There are consequences to your actions (choices and decisions).
25. Beware of the unintended consequences of your actions.
26. Watch your expectations of others. They are only human and will let you down if you expect them to be perfect.

27. If you want to receive loyalty, you must first be loyal to others.
28. Be considerate of others with your actions.
29. Treat other people's property as you want others to treat yours.
30. Just because someone has something you don't have; doesn't mean they are rich.
31. Even if they are rich, it is no excuse for abusing them or their property.
32. Be patient. Nothing is free, and you have to pay dues to reap the rewards in life.
33. Most rich and successful people paid their dues. Learn from them, but don't envy them.
34. Feelings of anger and envy don't hurt the other person half as much as they hurt you, because they prevent you from focusing and achieving positive results.
35. Strive for excellence in ALL things.
36. To be an effective leader, you must also be a good follower.
37. Be honest. ALWAYS tell the truth. People will forgive a mistake, but will never trust a liar.
38. What you think is what you feel. THINK POSITIVE!
39. Revere the past. The wisdom of the ages is at your fingertips.
40. There are two types of people: Those who look for ways to make things happen, and those who look for reasons why things can't happen. They both achieve what they see.
41. Former coach of the Carolina Panthers, Dom Capers, has a great philosophy. It is:

    Expect Nothing
    Work Hard
    Prepare for the worst
    Hope for the best

42. Be creative. Always be thinking of ways to improve yourself and/or the things you're doing.
43. Make friends with as many people as possible. Those relationships are the most important thing in life next to your relationship with God and your family. If you have friends and you are a true friend in return, you will be able to have a wide range of opportunities during your life.

God bless Texas! God bless the USA! We are blessed by being able to live in the greatest area in the world. This country doesn't owe you anything. If you want something, be prepared to earn it.

The Lessons Opened

"Life is not about expecting, hoping and wishing. It's about doing, being and becoming. It's about learning from the mistakes of others. You can't live long enough to make them all yourself."

—Eleanor Roosevelt

1

God exists! Have faith! Pray! Listen!

There is no question this lesson must be first because wherever we place our faith is the bedrock of our character.

My faith, belief, and hope are stronger than ever because of the many instances God has shown up in my life since I wrote the letter to John. Awakening me in the middle of the night with specific language to write, answered prayers, and interactions with others, He affirms my mission by having people contact me out of the blue, thanking me for something I wrote or said.

If we slow down, become still, and listen, we will hear Him speak to us in our spirit, through others, and in our surroundings. When we realize He has touched us, we are humbled, encouraged, and gain confidence in His promises for us.

I wish I had trusted Him more entirely and earlier. He wants us to enrich our lives to fulfill His purpose for us. He will provide for us what we need if we trust in him. **Isaiah 40:31** says, "But those who **hope** in the Lord will renew their strength. They will soar on wings like eagles; they will run and not grow weary; they will walk and not be faint."

May you discover His love for you and enjoy His presence fully in your life.

Hebrews 11:6

And without faith it is impossible to please God, because anyone who comes to him must believe that he exists and that he rewards those who earnestly seek him.

How This Lesson Applies to Me

____

____

____

____

2

Love and care for your mother!

You will be the man of the house. She unconditionally loves you and deserves your love, respect, and attention.

I told John this every time I left the house and carried it forward with Elizabeth after John passed. While men have a special responsibility to respect and protect women, the charge to do so extends to all.

I know they were both too young to understand it as infants, but I wanted to ingrain into their subconscious a sense of family responsibility that is stronger than other relationships.

Our culture disparages parents and the traditional family, which is essential to strong families and nations. Children understanding their place in their immediate and extended family supersedes their position in the world.

Parents' unconditional love is greater than children receive anywhere and provides them a protective shield against all threats. Conversely, the first commandment addressing interpersonal relations in Exodus 20:12 commands us to honor our parents.

As one whose mother has passed on, I'll never believe I repaid her love, sacrifice, and devotion to our family and me.

I hope you will experience the beauty of a mother's love and the delight of a wonderful family.

Exodus 20:12

Honor your father and your mother, so that you may live long in the land the Lord your God is giving you.

How This Lesson Applies to Me

____

____

____

____

3

Learn early, learn often, NEVER stop learning!

It will determine the level of your success.

The earlier you adopt this philosophy and the more dedicated you are to exercising it will exponentially multiply your achievements. If, for whatever reason, you fail to begin early, start at your earliest opportunity, and prioritize making up for lost time on every possible occasion.

Formal schooling can provide you with a foundation, and hopefully the ability to learn and think for yourself. But the self-education you gain after your school years through study, experience, and observation will benefit you most.

There are terrific lessons from our successes and even more from our setbacks and adversities if we seek to learn from them rather than just merely living our experiences.

We never know where or when a lesson that will dramatically change our journey and impact will occur. Ralph Waldo Emerson wisely said, "The mind, once stretched by a new idea, never returns to its original dimension." The great thing about life is we can repeatedly stretch our mind and benefit from continuous learning until our last breath.

In addition, the example we set for our family and friends will create a ripple effect, causing immeasurable influence on future generations living beyond our lifetimes.

Don't waste a day. Don't waste a minute. Begin NOW, and at the end of each day, you'll be amazed at the expansion of your efforts.

Proverbs 18:15 - The heart of the discerning acquires knowledge, for the ears of the wise seek it out.

How This Lesson Applies to Me

4

Remember: You learn more from your mistakes than your successes.

I've been blessed to realize many achievements and received enough grace to cover my poor choices and adversities. As I advocated in the previous lesson, life-long learning is essential to benefit from both types of experiences.

Humanity's instinct is to believe success comes from knowing everything needed to accomplish any given feat. Nothing could be further from the truth. Even in the most spectacular victories, lessons abound for future achievements; failure to learn them occurs due to pride. Admitting to others that they exist and that you will add them to your capabilities exhibits humility, which will endear those on your team and encourage others to join you for future triumphs.

On the other side of the ledger are setbacks and adversity resulting from poor choices, failure, mistakes, and the vagaries of life. The learning possibilities from negative experiences are virtually limitless.

An unknown person brilliantly said, "If you're going to make a mistake, make sure each one is a new one." People typically ask "why me?" when they experience suffering or adversity. I've come to believe it is the wrong question. It looks in the past, focuses only on oneself, and may trap us unable to progress into the future if we allow it to capture us.

I believe the proper question upon a mistake or negative ordeal is, "what now?" What lesson am I supposed to learn to grow and help others as I continue my journey? This question looks to the future, focuses on service to others, and opens the door for God to aid our recovery. I learned through John's death that when I focused on myself, I hurt more, and when I focused on helping others, I hurt less. My objective is to only experience one trial for a lesson, not more.

Regardless of the cause of our negative trial, there are many more lessons to learn and opportunities to grow for future service. Others will often look at our response to see if it is a worthy example to emulate when encountering tribulations.

Psalm 119:71
It was good for me to be afflicted so that
I might learn your decrees.

How This Lesson Applies to Me

____

____

____

____

5

ALWAYS HAVE A POSITIVE ATTITUDE.

Your individual personality and character will determine much of your attitude. How you respond to negative people and experiences, as discussed previously, will also influence your outlook on life.

Each of us chooses our point of view, and our choices affect everything on our journey. Henry Ford said, "Think you can, or think you can't. Either way, you'll be right."

The first thing impacted by our choice is the number and influence of our achievements. Nothing positive is ever accomplished with a negative attitude. If we want to achieve the highest level of success with our contributions to the world, we must believe we can realize our dreams.

The second impact also contributes to our attaining victory in our efforts. No one wants to be around people who constantly hold a negative attitude. Life is hard enough without the people around you adding resistance to your endeavors. People want to associate with winners. When you're positive, you appear confident, and you will attract others to aid your causes.

The third impact is on your health and life span. Viktor Frankl wrote *Man's Search for Meaning* about his experience in Nazi concentration camps in World War II. He discovered man's last freedom was choosing how to respond to the most horrible situations. Those who reacted with positive attitudes survived the camps and war at a significantly higher rate than those who viewed every experience negatively.

Philippians 4:8

Finally, brothers and sisters, whatever is true, whatever is noble, whatever is right, whatever is pure, whatever is lovely, whatever is admirable—if anything is excellent or praiseworthy—think about such things.

How This Lesson Applies to Me

____

____

____

____

6

Don't speak ill of others

There is no doubt this is a tough principle by which to live. Our nature is to speak before we think and say what is on our minds.

The time-honored adage passed through generations by wise grandmothers says, "If you can't say something nice about someone, don't say anything." It is as accurate today as eternally.

Another truism is: If you do speak ill about another, expect them to discover what you said. I know this from experience when I failed to heed this advice, which is why I included it.

Compounding the issue is that when we speak ill behind a person's back to others, they will automatically magnify our words. Most likely, our words will be embellished by others before reaching the subject's ears. Correcting misstatements and healing the offended person's heart is painful, difficult, takes time at best, and may never be possible.

What we say about others is another vital part of our character. If people hear us speak ill of others, they can be sure that we will talk unfavorably about them at some time. I once worked for a man who criticized every person who left the company, and their performance or reason for departing didn't matter. It was apparent that he would also speak similarly about me when I left the organization. The late actress Audrey Hepburn said, "You can tell more about what a person says about others than what others say about him."

James 3:5 (TLB) sums it up:
The tongue is a small thing, but what
enormous damage it can do.

Proverbs 15:4
The soothing tongue is a tree of life,
but a perverse tongue crushes the spirit.

How This Lesson Applies to Me

____

____

____

____

7

Don't listen to negativism

It is a cancer that will deter you from success.

I may sound like a broken record as I emphasize optimism repeatedly in different ways in the letter.

However, the world, the way events are reported in the world, and I dare say, a majority of people emit negativism around the clock.

We choose what we feed our body physically, mentally, and spiritually daily. We will thrive if we consume nourishing food and exercise, information to stimulate our minds and endeavors, and soul-saving spiritual lessons. Our efforts will provide positive examples for others, achieve our maximum success, and provide a foundation benefitting our family for future generations.

Norman Vincent Peale advised, "You must feed your mind even as you feed your body, and to make your mind healthy, you must feed it nourishing wholesome thoughts."

Choosing positive people with whom to associate for work, friendships, and other relationships is just as important. Positive people will be great examples for us, lift our spirits, encourage the pursuit of our dreams, and care for us in our darkest hours.

On the other hand, if we feed our minds with negative news, gossip, pop-culture nonsense, discouraging relationships, and milquetoast spirituality, it will be easy for our attitude to drift or fall into a pessimistic viewpoint. Wherever we are, the moment we succumb to negative thinking will limit our achievement in life because a positive attitude is essential to all accomplishments.

I've seen examples of family and friends' lives derailed by defeatism and hopelessness. They may continue to live physically, but mentally and spiritually, they are the walking dead because they exist without hope, joy, or enthusiasm.

Finally, if you don't believe me, maybe you'll accept someone who overcame monumental challenges, failures, and discouragement. Albert Einstein revolutionized our view of time and space and achieved several scientific discoveries we're still learning from today, including the most famous theory of relativity. He warned us to, "Stay away from negative people. They have a problem for every solution."

Proverbs 14:7
Stay away from a fool, for you will
not find knowledge on their lips.

How This Lesson Applies to Me

____

____

____

____

8

Smile. Say please and thank you.

Yes, this seems so obvious it is hardly worth mentioning. However, in my experience, seldom do people regularly exercise these simple displays of common courtesy.

Years ago, a radio disc jockey at WBAP in Ft. Worth would sign off the air saying, "Keep smiling! Make the world wonder what you've been up to." I always thought it was great advice because even a little smile communicates happiness and invites the recipient in for a conversation.

Smiling can also exude enthusiasm and confidence in success, attracting people to us because everyone wants to associate with winners.

Growing up, my parents, and I'll bet most of yours, used a technical term to teach me politeness. When I wanted something and asked for it, they asked, "What's the magic word?" At first, I didn't know, and they instructed me to say please and repeated the process until it became my second nature.

Unfortunately, we often forget the power we extend to others and receive back from them from this straightforward expression. It is deplorable in interactions with people who serve us one way or another. It can be easy for the recipient to understand the request as a command without respect given to them. Adding please to the end of a request grants the recipient respect and elevates their station to one more equal with the requestor. I've always felt more respected by individuals at every level in society when I extended them respect first.

Saying thank you goes together with please, like peanut butter and jelly. Again, it is simple, but how often do people omit this expression in their daily interactions?

One day, discussing these topics in a radio interview, the interviewer asked me about responses to saying thank you. Without thinking, I said, "I've never had a bad experience saying thank you." We laughed, but it is universally true. If we're thankful for something that is done for us, how can we have a negative experience saying thank you?

Richard Branson said, "Please be polite. Nothing in life should erode the habit of saying thank you to people or praising them."

It doesn't take a scientific survey to confirm that if you will smile, and say please and thank you that you will enjoy a richer life and receive respect and friendship from many more people.

1 Thessalonians 5:18
Give thanks in all circumstances; for this
is God's will for you in Christ Jesus.

How This Lesson Applies to Me

____

____

____

____

9

Be sincere.

This is another recommendation that appears to be a no-brainer but isn't. It's unbelievable to me how often people interact with others insincerely.

I initially recognized disingenuous behavior in the business world during my first corporate position out of college. I was a green sales rep. Most of the management team treated me equally, except for one service manager, several years older than me. He considered me second-class and never missed an opportunity to ensure I knew it.

Three years after joining the business, the company promoted me to a sales manager position and relocated me to Alabama. At the next management meeting, I encountered the service manager who now treated me like the Duke of Corporatelandia. I was astonished but learned a valuable lesson: We never know when people below us today will be above us tomorrow.

Some people treat others differently based on their perceived or actual power and wealth, which is true in business and personal relationships. I believe this behavior is worse now because the emphasis on materialism and power over honor and principle is more significant than at any time in my life. It is shallow and short-sighted.

Untold numbers of television shows and movies utilize a con where people show power and money to lure others into a position to be scammed. Men and women play games regarding their wealth, status, power, age, and other parameters, intent on misleading the other party.

We need to be an expert in discernment as the Native Americans who discriminated against people who spoke with what they called a "forked tongue" (insincere, untruthful) and valued individuals who spoke with a "straight tongue" (sincere, truthful, trustworthy).

If we treat everyone sincerely, equally, and respectfully, from the lowest person to the highest, we will never be in an embarrassing situation. We'll get along better with everyone and find more doors open for us to pursue our dreams. We will also better defend ourselves against scams as we improve our skills in reading others' actions, which are immensely more important than their statements.

Additionally, when people recognize our sincerity, they will trust us more easily because they know what we say to their face is the same thing we'll speak to anyone behind their back.

James 3:17

But the wisdom that comes from heaven is first of all pure; then peace-loving, considerate, submissive, full of mercy and good fruit, impartial and sincere.

HOW THIS LESSON APPLIES TO ME

____

____

____

____

10

Be on time!

Tardiness is one of my pet peeves because the tardy person reveals a lack of respect and consideration for the time of whomever they delay.

When we establish a reputation for showing up on time, others will strive to arrive at the pre-planned time also. Both parties win in this case, and their relationship is one of mutual respect.

We all have exceptions when we can't arrive on time for an appointment. Everyone understands that, especially if we communicate that we will be late.

What is infuriating is people who perpetually show up late and enter a room expecting applause and fanfare. Their action says, "My time is more important than yours."

Rob Nalley, an executive whom I worked under, said, "Better never than late." Rob taught interrupting an ongoing meeting by arriving late demonstrates a lack of consideration of others' time twice.

As a leader, begin and end every meeting on time as a sign of respect! When we consistently start on time, people will respond, and more will show up on schedule. When we end meetings as planned or earlier, it will enhance our leadership status with the team.

If we begin and end meetings late, people will disrespect our leadership more in all areas.

Simply said, disrespecting others' time results in them dishonoring us.

Romans 13:7

Give to everyone what you owe them: If you owe taxes, pay taxes; if revenue, then revenue; if respect, then respect; if honor, then honor.

How This Lesson Applies to Me

____

____

____

____

11

Be humble!

The tendency of human nature we see displayed daily is to boast and celebrate achievement, which focuses exclusively on self and now. Life is tough, and there is no sense in making it more challenging by turning people off with an arrogant attitude regardless of our success.

Life is full of ups and downs, and today's success is no guarantee we will always be successful. If we're humble when we are on top of the world, we will experience better treatment on those dreaded days when we experience setbacks and adversity.

The old cowboys said, "There has never been a horse that can't be rode, and there's never been a rider who can't be throwed."

If we are always humble in our attitude and behavior, we will appear even-tempered, not revealing our current state of life. If we are thankful for what we have every day, if we are considerate of others, and if we focus on the long view of life, friends will celebrate our victories and lift our spirits when we suffer defeat.

As one who experienced the highest highs and lowest lows, Winston Churchill said, "In War: Resolution. In Defeat: Defiance. In Victory: Magnanimity. In Peace: Good Will."

Merriam Webster defines magnanimous as "showing or suggesting nobility of feeling and generosity of mind." It indeed excludes boasting, bragging, in-your-face celebrations, and any action demeaning to others.

Take the long view of life. Appreciate what you have. Celebrate victory as if you have won before, and endure defeat knowing you will overcome it and win again.

Matthew 23:12

For those who exalt themselves will be humbled,
and those who humble themselves will be exalted.

How This Lesson Applies to Me

____

____

____

____

12

Keep your word!

We build our reputation over a lifetime, but one statement or act can instantly destroy it. How others see us is a reflection of our parents, grandparents, and forbearers. It is also an introduction to our descendants.

In his highly acclaimed *The Seven Habits of Highly Effective People*, Stephen Covey suggested we visualize how we wanted people to think of us at our funeral. He proposed we control that future reality with every decision we make until then. When we disregard pop culture to do what feels good, and calculate our actions based on others' views of our character at life's end, we will always make better decisions!

Early in my business career, it was common for corporations to conduct business with a person's word and a handshake. If there was a problem with a deal, both parties worked it out honorably and fairly. Unfortunately, too many people's short-sightedness, selfishness, and greed led to our current world of lawyers' involvement with every agreement and ever-increasing litigation.

In personal and business actions, electronic communications allow people to hide, thinking others will not discover their dishonorable acts. Whether we communicate face-to-face, verbally, through formally written documents, or in brief electronic messages, we are accountable for our word and reputation.

Every indication is that the masses will continue to think only of themselves and the moment instead of the long-term adverse effects of their disreputable behavior. They prove Aesop's statement, "After all is said and done, more is said than done."

If we commit to do something, we should fulfill our commitment. As I've told my team members, "I did is better than I will."

The resulting good news is that if others see us as the exception who keep our word in all matters, we will stand out, and the doors of opportunity will open widely for us.

1 Corinthians 4:2
Now it is required that those who have been
given a trust must prove faithful.

How This Lesson Applies to Me

____

____

____

____

13

Be proactive!

It is easy to sit back and wait for a more perfect time to act on any endeavor. Pop culture, human nature, and previous unsuccessful actions incentivize us to avoid the risk of future failure from our proactive efforts.

Some people look for ways to make things happen, but a more significant number of people rationalize reasons for their inaction. Only those who step out of their comfort zone have the opportunity to grow beyond their present status.

Hyrum W. Smith said, "To reach any goal, you must leave your comfort zone." Discomfort is a requirement for progress. The good news is every time we overcome uneasiness, it elevates our comfort level thereby building our confidence to face future opportunities.

To succeed in life, we must persist in pursuing our dreams until our last breath. It is no shame to depart this life in the process of future achievement, but it is regrettable to rest on our laurels when the additional effort produces more fruit, benefitting people today and beyond our lifetimes.

Thomas Edison was the most prolific inventor of the 20th century holding 1,093 patents, which resulted from his proactivity and unwavering persistence.

Edison's most famous inventions include a reliable incandescent light bulb, the phonograph, Fluoroscopy for x-rays, film, Kinetoscope for moving pictures, the phonograph cylinder for voice recording, and more than 1,000 more.

When asked about why it took him so long to improve light bulb reliability, Edison said, "I have not failed. I just found 10,000 ways that didn't work."

Each of us benefits every day from proactive efforts and refusal to quit in the face of failure.

When in doubt, Act!

1 John 3:18
Dear children, let us not love with words
or speech but with actions and in truth.

How This Lesson Applies to Me

____

____

____

____

14

You will make mistakes. Don't be afraid.

Making mistakes in life is perfectly natural, as is the fear of future mistakes that follow. Each of us is our worst critic upon a setback. Well-meaning friends and others less well-intentioned add to our displeasure. No one feels worse in a ball game than the person who let their teammates down. Criticizing them adds to their pain. Telling them they will succeed next time, and further encouragement will lift their spirit and position them for future victory.

As painful as our mistakes are, the pain of regret from not pursuing a desired dream or goal is more hurtful and lasts far longer. I can attest to this personally, and if you minimize your lifetime regrets from this message, I will succeed in my warning.

History's greatest successes all overcame several failures. Household names you wouldn't know if they succumbed to their fear of failure and didn't persevere in their endeavors include The Wright Brothers, Walt Disney, Abraham Lincoln, Albert Einstein, Oprah Winfrey, J.K. Rowling, and innumerable others.

Many people have stated a variation of the following statement, and they're all correct, "It's not how many times you get knocked down in life that counts, but how many times you get back up."

It is essential we don't allow mistakes to deter our continued growth, action, and success in life. If we cease our quest for future accomplishments, we sentence ourselves permanently to where we presently reside.

Robert T. Kiyosaki confirms this reality by not permitting mistakes to deter our endeavors saying, "The reason so many people fail to achieve success is because they fail to fail enough times."

Isaiah 41:10

So do not fear, for I am with you; do not be dismayed, for I am your God. I will strengthen you and help you; I will uphold you with my righteous right hand.

How This Lesson Applies to Me

____

____

____

____

15

Can't never did anything.

This gem is another precious lesson from my father; though I was slow to grasp it, it has provided invaluable inspiration over a lifetime. As Dad taught me innumerable skills in life, he regularly pushed me to my limit and beyond.

Working on any project or chore beyond my skill level as a youngster led to a defeatist attitude. Frustrated, I would exclaim, "I can't do that!" His quick, demonstrative, and confident responses always were, "Can't never did anything!" The comment produced further frustration because it meant the exercise wasn't over but would continue until I mastered the task. Thank goodness he didn't permit his annoyance with my failure to deter his persistence. Once learned, the lesson and attitude continue to benefit me daily.

I wrote of Jen Bricker in *Navigating Life's Journey*. She was born in 1987 without legs, and her birth parents put her up for adoption. Her adoptive parents raised her identically to their other children.

The only rule was that she "never say the word can't!" Her dad taught her tumbling and the trampoline when she was age seven. Jen's desire to lead a normal life and accomplish feats beyond others' expectations created a fire inside her soul. She earned a state championship in power tumbling and played high school softball and basketball.

Now married, she is a professional acrobat, aerialist, speaker, and author of *Everything is Possible*. Her story inspires us to attempt more, retreat less, and never quit chasing our dreams.

Michael Hyatt instructs us, "You can't fail if you don't quit. You can't succeed if you don't start."

It is imperative to pursue every endeavor to success or failure. Doing so will lead us to greater heights of performance, and our setbacks will provide us with the seeds for success in other enterprises.

Mark 9:23
"'If you can?'" said Jesus. "Everything is possible for one who believes."

How This Lesson Applies to Me

____

____

____

____

16

There is ALWAYS an alternative choice.

Like everyone, I have made some good choices, and too many I regret. The key is learning the proper lesson from every poor decision as quickly as possible to avoid repeating it in the future.

It is also imperative that we aren't short-sighted in evaluating options. Too often, we limit our alternatives based on previous experience, lack of knowledge, not availing ourselves of counsel, or other reasons. That results in limited choices, increasing our likelihood of repeated failure and regret.

It is common for us to focus only on one side of an issue when considering our choices. I like to utilize an equation to illustrate looking at alternatives from multiple sides to determine our best choice in a matter.

My sales reps used to complain about their compensation plans because they wanted to make more money, and I replied that every equation has two sides. They insisted the company revise their compensation when selling more and reducing personal expenses were valid but non-preferred alternatives.

We make hundreds of choices every day. Some have immediate results, others impact us later, and the consequences last longer. The good news is we can change course upon discovering a poor choice. The earlier we do so, the lesser the cost and penalty will be for ourselves and everyone affected by our decision.

Identifying maximum alternatives before a choice, sound decision-making logic, and contingency planning in case of a setback reduces our likelihood of long-term failure. Kenneth Burke affirms the difficulty in the decision process, saying, "If decisions were a choice between alternatives, decisions would come easy. Decision is the selection and formulation of alternatives."

If Burke is correct, contingency planning adds another layer to the decision process. How many alternatives should we plan if plan A fails? Chris Guillebeau advises, "If plan A fails, remember there are 25 more letters."

One thing is sure, the better we stretch our minds thinking of options, the better choice we will make initially, the more contingent alternatives we will discover, and the greater the odds of our success.

Proverbs 12:26
The righteous choose their friends carefully,
but the way of the wicked leads them astray.

How This Lesson Applies to Me

___

___

___

___

17

You don't have to know everything, but you do have to know enough to keep from being taken advantage of.

Another gem from Papaw Battle

What my father said in down-home Texan is called *discernment* by others. Dictionary.com defines it as "the faculty of discerning; discrimination; acuteness of judgment and understanding."

But I thought discrimination was a bad thing! In another context, yes, but discriminating between good and bad choices, hearing the truth or a mistruth, judging people's behavior toward us, and in many other areas is essential to smoothing our journey in life.

Discernment is rarely learned in the classroom or in books, but more often in the school of hard knocks. The wisest people I've known in life weren't the best educated, but whose understanding of human nature, common sense, and people skills were unrivaled.

On the other hand, I've known some well-schooled individuals who could barely walk and chew gum simultaneously. The late comedian Jerry Clower said it best; addressing a lady who thought she was superior to everyone else, he said, "It's obvious you've been educated beyond your intelligence."

Naiveté is also another symptom of one not possessing discernment. I had a sales rep work for me years ago selling into the automotive dealer market who told me one day, "I have to believe what dealer X told me because he said it was so." I had to counsel him dealers were sometimes like politicians, defining the truth as whatever helped them win the deal they were negotiating.

When receiving information that sounds far-fetched, we have to intercept it as untruthful, ask for additional proof, and hold judgment until the communicator proves our initial reading incorrect.

My objectives and recommendations for others are to be lifelong learners, in and out of the classroom. Study human nature, observe and learn from others' past and present, and hone our discernment for a more successful and fulfilling life.

Proverbs 1:7
The fear of the LORD is the beginning of knowledge,
but fools despise wisdom and instruction.

HOW THIS LESSON APPLIES TO ME

____

____

____

____

18

YOU ARE NO BETTER AND NO WORSE THAN ANYONE ELSE.

What a puzzling world we live in!

God created us equal, and our Declaration of Independence acknowledges that "all men are created equal, endowed by their Creator with certain unalienable Rights, among these are life, liberty, and the pursuit of happiness."

However, individually we possess gifts others don't, and others are blessed with skills absent from us. Our human nature and ego influence us to believe we're better than others when we demonstrate our talents. Similarly, others using their abilities can cause feelings of inferiority or envy if we don't understand and respect the uniqueness of every individual.

Terrible discrimination and treatment have been and still are perpetrated against people because of their race, religion, sex, nationality, position in life, and other reasons because of man's imperfections. Even if we're mistreated for one reason, our instinct is to believe we are still better than others.

When we recognize and accept every person's uniqueness and utilize our gifts for the purpose God intended for us, we can fulfill our destiny and respect others doing likewise.

Then, we can live each day treating others with the golden rule, "Do unto others as you would have them do unto you," and thicken our skin for mistreatment from others who haven't yet recognized this principle.

The person robbing us at gunpoint is the obvious example of someone ignoring the golden rule and violating laws and norms to increase their station at the expense of their victim.

Too many people in the 21st century whine and cry with the least offensive "triggers" while others withstand withering actions from despicable people without muttering a word in response.

If we judge people based on "the content of their character, not the color of their skin" or any other characteristic, as Martin Luther King Jr. admonished, we will treat others better, and I bet they will do the same for us in most cases.

Genesis 1:27

So God created mankind in his own image, in the image of God he created them; male and female he created them.

How This Lesson Applies to Me

____

____

____

____

19

BE VERY GRATEFUL FOR WHAT YOU HAVE.

It doesn't take long to find someone worse off than you are.

There are two opposing views of life played out in different ways. People think they can do something or think they can't, and both are correct. They are happy in life or not. They are optimistic or pessimistic. They love or they hate.

The application of this message is seen in our viewpoint about what we have in life. Our culture promotes jealousy and envy of what others have that we don't. It is a straightforward philosophy because no one has everything, and we can always discover someone else who has what we desire.

This mindset leads to perpetual misery, regardless of what we have or acquire in our lifetime. Expectations to achieve something unattainable destine us for unhappiness.

Rarer, but a better philosophy, to attain contentment is appreciating what we have regardless of how large or small it is. We can always find someone worse off than we are, and our gratitude for our good fortune is appropriate.

Most of us know someone who has more than most people, but constantly strives for even more and never achieves happiness. Conversely, it surprises people to observe people who don't have much but live lives of happiness because they recognize it isn't what you have in life that makes you happy, but how you view what you possess.

The apostle Paul suffered mightily for his faith in God. He was beaten, shipwrecked, flogged, imprisoned, and experienced many trials. Despite the opportunity to complain, he stated in the book to the Philippians he had learned to be content in all circumstances. His attitude enabled him to endure his suffering and serve as a fantastic example for us.

We hear stories of school custodians or others who pass, leaving behind vast fortunes despite always living below their meager means. It validates that our earthly possessions don't buy happiness; we can be happy with much or little based on our response to what life delivers us.

Philippians 4:12-13

I know what it is to be in need, and I know what it is to have plenty. I have learned the secret of being content in any and every situation, whether well fed or hungry, whether living in plenty or in want. I can do all this through him who gives me strength.

Colossians 2: 6b-7

...continue to live your lives in him, rooted and built up in him, strengthened in the faith as you were taught, and overflowing with thankfulness.

How This Lesson Applies to Me

____

____

____

____

20

Have a sense of humor.

Things are never as bad as they appear. A sense of humor will lighten most situations.

Humor is more important now than ever as we see people more easily offended than at any other time in memory. When people are secure in their skin and confident, it is much more challenging to offend them with mere words.

My parents raised me with the principle, "Sticks and stones may break my bones, but words will never hurt me." When someone said something mean, Dad and Mom taught us to buck up and let it roll off our sleeves.

The spirit of a humorous comment is as vital as the comment itself. If someone uses humor to attack us, it is significantly different than if they are kidding us. It seems people have lost the ability to distinguish the difference today, which is a loss for everyone.

Our ability to hear a disparaging comment and not show it hurts us demonstrates to the transgressor they failed. They are less likely to attack us again if they were unsuccessful in their first attempt. On the other hand, if we reveal pain and suffering from their insult, we will invite further and escalating abuse.

True before and true now, "laughter is the best medicine" with most things in life. I believe there is something humorous in most things if we take the time to look for it.

If we can laugh at ourselves when others poke fun at us, it will demonstrate our confidence and humility. If we can also utilize self-deprecating humor, poking fun at ourselves, we enhance our spirit, and others elevate their view of us. Both traits are endearing to others, allowing them to relax in our presence and be genuine.

Except in the most tragic of losses, humor relieves pressure and stress. Thankfully, I found humor even in my cancer treatments, enabling me to endure them more easily. Sharing that humor with others, I believe, provided an excellent example of life and faith regardless of what the future will bring.

Job 8:21
He will yet fill your mouth with laughter
and your lips with shouts of joy.

How This Lesson Applies to Me

____

____

____

____

21

Anyone can do the things they like.

Those who do the things they must do, but don't want to do will have greater success than the majority.

If you want to achieve higher-than-average results, take on the challenging assignments and responsibilities no one wants.

Many people complete their easiest projects first, postponing the less desirable tasks as long as possible. They hope someone else will pick up their slack, or the burden will fade away. It very rarely does.

In the meantime, they live in fear of the chore they dread, which zaps their peace and energy. The pressure to face undesirable activities incentivizes us to choose shorter-term alternatives to provide immediate pressure relief.

I've learned to accept responsibility for undertakings I don't desire because it will provide me with growth, differentiate me from others, and open doors to more appealing opportunities in the future.

When I tackle the most demanding tasks first, I get them out of the way and exceed the expectations of all involved in the enterprise. Completing the most challenging activities provides me peace, relieves stress, and even makes the easier chores less burdensome.

An additional benefit arrives with the completion of each challenging mission. I become more confident in my abilities to scale future mountains, which always appear over the horizon.

Organization leaders quickly identify people they can trust and rely upon during difficult days. There is always room for those people in any institution or group because they are critical to team success.

Our everyday choices, large and small, personal and business, short-term and lifetime, give us the immediate results of our actions and unseen impacts that can continue beyond our lifetimes.

If we lengthen our perspective before facing difficult circumstances, we're more likely to choose better paths, leading to happier and more successful lives for us and those who follow us.

Proverbs 14:23
All hard work brings a profit,
but mere talk leads only to poverty.

How This Lesson Applies to Me

____

____

____

____

22

The "easy way out" is usually only easy in the short run.

When the pressure of adversity smacks us in the face, our natural response is to try to escape. We frantically search for the "easy way out" that provides us with the quickest relief. There is always one choice that appears right in front of our eyes.

In youth, before we have the experience that judgment brings, we seize the quick, easy escape and feel the confidence resulting from our decision. It is generally only a matter of time before reality strikes us on the other cheek, and we find the original problem compounded by our actions.

Quicker choices are often more emotional than rational, and life events teach us deliberate and rational selections from alternatives almost always improve our future. When we relent to pressure and feelings that push aside logic, we usually regret the result once the smoke clears.

I've often said the "easy way out" is an oxymoron because its apparent benefit is usually a mirage and only provides temporary relief. Unfortunately, the primary source that teaches us this truth is a personal experience instead of observing others' misfortunes.

Make it your practice to learn from the lives of others by observation and study to minimize the pain of personal setbacks.

Proverbs 14:17
A quick-tempered person does foolish things,
and the one who devises evil schemes is hated.

How This Lesson Applies to Me

____

____

____

____

23

Think before you act.

This is another piece of advice that is easy to overlook because it seems so apparent! In theory, we believe we think before we act all the time. In practice, especially when we're younger, we impulsively act or react more often than we should.

I believe it is a combination of thinking that we're more thoughtful if we act quickly, our expediency will reward us, and/or we want to check something off our list to progress to something more appealing.

Current culture exponentially adds pressure for us to respond to text and email messages faster than we should, and we soon expect others to reply almost instantaneously to our communications as well.

In reality, most issues requiring activity from us will not worsen if we give ourselves and others additional time to think and process alternative answers and responses. Not only will we make better decisions, but those we communicate with will be relieved to take more time and provide us with better action also.

Napoleon Bonaparte was famous for only looking at his mail once every three weeks. His theory was small matters would be solved by subordinates, and questions requiring his personal attention would remain for him to address. He rarely experienced a penalty with his system and believed it benefitted everyone. I'm not advocating a three-week delay in today's world but balancing our time to allow reason over expediency will almost always help us.

Davy Crockett's advice was similar and simple, "Be sure you're right, then go ahead." It's similar to the *Stop, Look, and Listen* signs that adorned railroad crossings before lights and crossing arms were installed. Crockett's advice slows us down enough to provide us with an opportunity to minimize making a poor decision.

Crockett's philosophy was purely American, fitting our individual liberties and rugged individualism. Since we have freedom over so many areas of our lives, it is our responsibility to make well-reasoned choices. Failure to do so threatens our success and imperils our republic.

So, the next time an issue confronts you, step back, consider your alternatives, contemplate their short and long-term implications, and go ahead confident you made the best possible selection available to you.

Proverbs 21:2
A person may think their own ways are right,
but the Lord weighs the heart.

How This Lesson Applies to Me

____

____

____

____

24

There are consequences to your actions (choices and decisions).

Yes, our actions and decisions can produce good and bad results and consequences. My purpose is to warn of the effects of poor choices and motivate you to consistently make the best long-term decisions.

Our culture is appealing and inviting to our human nature, but it teams with attractive opportunities leading to destructive lives and eternity. It motivates us to forget the past, move quickly in the present, and not worry about the future.

“What happens in Vegas stays in Vegas” is one of the most seductive advertising campaigns in my lifetime, which is so good, many people buy into it despite its 100% falsehood. Especially with the vast array and proximity of 21st-century technology, someone will most likely communicate everything we say and do to the world, both during and beyond our lifetime.

Thus, it is imperative for our good character, reputation, and well-being to make selections we won’t regret and that will not constrain the pursuit of our dreams.

The mad rush beginning in 2020 to “cancel” individuals and pull down statues of 19th-century heroes because of one transgression should serve as an example of consequences occurring long after we leave the planet. It makes no difference if our actions are acceptable today and our contemporaries celebrate us. Imagine a devolved culture in the 22nd century that cancels the entire population of capitalists, socialists, people who worked for a living, one gender, one race, or any other category under the sun that they find offensive in their day! I would have never believed it possible before our recent experiences.

Many of the changes in American culture since 2009 were unimaginable prior to that time. People insisting on the existence of more than two genders, the trans movement, and marriage within the same sex are a few of the massive transformations we have witnessed.

So how can we live prosperously today and minimize our likelihood of embarrassing our descendants?

First, we must choose principles and values based on the truth that has survived, thrived, and proven worthy over the millennia. Yes, I'm Christian, and I believe in Jesus' statement that He is "the way, the truth, and the life, and no one comes to the Father except through me," as taught in John 14.

Second, we will fare better in life if we resist the siren song of popular culture and choose alternatives based on their effects on our lifetime and beyond. Most of my failures resulted from making rushed decisions in the moment instead of taking the time to make deliberate choices and considering their impact on my entire life and beyond.

Contrary to conventional wisdom, there is always a consequence and impact of our decisions and choices, and we'll enjoy the journey much better when we routinely choose wisely.

Proverbs 22:3

The prudent see danger and take refuge,
but the simple keep going and pay the penalty.

How This Lesson Applies to Me

____

____

____

____

25

Beware of the unintended consequences of your actions.

Another crucial, but different facet of thinking before we act, (as discussed in number 23), is considering ALL of the possible *unintended* consequences of our decisions.

When I was younger and less experienced, I prided myself on my quick decisions. Painfully and too slowly, I realized good long-term choices were better for me and everyone involved rather than the rapidity of my previous conclusions.

Yes, most of my preferences were beneficial for a while. As time passed and people responded to my actions, I determined other alternatives were better long-term choices. Finally, I learned to think and consider how my decisions would stand the test of time, which has ultimately led to better results.

As life exposed me to more complex issues, I soon learned to consider precedence and example in my decisions. These two considerations are essential in selecting the optimum choices for maximum success.

The next unseen trap I discovered in the decision process was the unintended consequences of my choices based on parameters I overlooked, as well as the responses of those affected by my actions. Those unexpected consequences, which we see all too often from politicians with little real-world experience, led me to a more deliberative and broad-based decision process, gladly sacrificing quickness for consistent achievement.

When I was in the Jaycees, our project planning tool titled the Chairman's Planning Guide (CPG) demanded we anticipate unintended consequences. The post-project portion of the plan required listing unanticipated problems and how we overcame them. That question benefitted the project's leaders the subsequent year and developed a thought process of proactively thinking and anticipating any problem we could envision ahead of time.

I read my favorite unanticipated problem while judging projects as part of the award program of the Jaycees. A West Texas chapter sponsored a parade where a goat was tied up in the bed of a pickup truck of one participant. The goat became excited and jumped over the edge of the bed, strangling himself until he expired. The chapter wrote they didn't anticipate that event, which they would next year, and coach parade floats on how to avoid similar tragedies.

In summary, the best decisions:

- Stand the test of time.
- Consider precedence on future issues.
- Consider the example they will set for future people.
- Consider the unintended consequences that may overwhelm the original intent of the alternative.

Romans 6:21

What benefit did you reap at that time from the things you are now ashamed of? Those things result in death!

HOW THIS LESSON APPLIES TO ME

____

____

____

____

26

Watch your expectations of others.

They are only human and will let you down if you expect them to be perfect.

Many of our greatest disappointments in life are a result of misplaced expectations.

We expect others to behave in specific ways and repeatedly experience the unexpected. We also periodically let others down.

Many times, we let others down due to some pressure we're experiencing. I wrote of the Frailty of Man in *Navigating Life's Journey: Common Sense in Uncommon Times,* saying:

"The Frailty of Man

Pressure that results from adversity reveals our character.
We all fail under pressure some of the time;
Some of us fail under pressure all of the time.
Thankfully, we all don't fail under pressure all of the time;
Those successes under pressure build our society and forge progress."

Former Carolina Panthers coach Dom Caper's philosophy places us in a place that minimizes disenchantment. I'll highlight it in lesson 41, but it says to "expect nothing."

Loyalty, trust, and love built over years, combined with successful experiences strengthen our commitment to meeting and exceeding others' expectations. The business slogan, "under promise and over deliver," serves personal relationships well also.

I'm blessed to have many friends who, through experience, exhibited steadfast friendship with me. I would trust my daughter Elizabeth's life to them. Even so, I know they may let me down or I them occasionally. Our relationship is deep enough to weather a letdown because of its infrequency and the vast number of positive trials we've endured.

Our goal is to be reliable, dependable, trustworthy, and loyal to friends, rarely disappointing them, hoping they aim likewise, and dealing with each other with compassion when we fall short.

Proverbs 11:7
Hopes placed in mortals die with them;
all the promise of their power comes to nothing.

How This Lesson Applies to Me

____

____

____

____

27

If you want to receive loyalty, you must first be loyal to others.

Too often, loyalty is ignored for winning an effort in the present. Marxism and other derivatives of its philosophy espouse "moral relativism" or "situational ethics" which advocates erasing past lessons, not worrying about the future, and using whomever you need to advance your position now.

The Christian faith cherishes truth, loyalty, trustworthiness, dependability, honor, devotion, and love between people through the ups and downs in life.

We extend loyalty to others and receive it from them along a continuum. The more we give first, the more we will receive in return, which is an essential biblical principle in all areas of life.

I have a handful of friends with whom I would entrust my family and possessions, and I hope I've earned that level of loyalty and trust with them.

How do we and our friends display our loyalty to earn such high esteem? My experience says how we walk together through difficult days and exercise dependability to overcome adversity is the only proof trustworthy for knowing how your friends will help you face future hardships.

People who have endured and survived combat together display a brotherhood, a certain closeness, trust, and loyalty that a crowbar can't dislodge. I've never experienced war, but I have shared tough times with friends who proved their fidelity and grit, to use the personality trait of the lead character in the movie and book, *True Grit*.

Benjamin Franklin summarized it best, "A friend in need is a friend indeed."

We must be that loyal friend who is always truthful, trustworthy, dependable, honorable, devoted, and loving. If we consistently live these values, we will receive the blessing of returned loyalty from others.

Because loyalty and its other derivatives are so crucial to life and eternity, I'm including two verses but could have added many more demonstrating Scripture's emphases.

Romans 12:10
Be devoted to one another in love.
Honor one another above yourselves.

Proverbs 17:17
A friend loves at all times, and a brother
is born for a time of adversity.

How This Lesson Applies to Me

____

____

____

____

28

Be considerate of others with your actions.

We all fail this advice occasionally, but the more we respect others by considering them in our actions, the more others will also honor us.

Yes, there are exceptions on both sides of anything but the majority of the time, consideration is met with returned consideration.

Like many other lessons, I wish I had also learned this one earlier. Too often, when we're younger, we barely consider the impact of our deeds on ourselves, much less on others. We act or react, and the consequences for us and others can be for better or, more often, for worse.

Basketball legend John Wooden taught, "Consider the rights of others before your own feelings, and the feelings of others before your own rights." We could benefit immensely by using that creed more in our culture today. We can easily see the results of ignoring this advice, and we can discover the beneficial effects of adopting it by studying our past.

Benjamin Franklin's advice, "When you're good to others, you're best to yourselves," adds the promise of a benefit more valuable than silver or gold by treating others well, which would include consideration. Franklin knew an attitude of service to others would automatically enhance one's life.

Zig Ziglar said it similarly, "You can get everything you want in life by helping enough other people get what they want." He recognized that considering and helping others achieve their dreams creates an army ready to help us in our hour of need.

Our human nature is to focus immediately and nearly always on our own desires. When we learn to defer self-fulfillment to benefit others, we see there is a natural satisfaction we realize whether or not they ever return the favor to us.

Matthew 7:12

So in everything, do to others what you would have them do to you, for this sums up the Law and the Prophets.

How This Lesson Applies to Me

____

____

____

____

29

Treat other people's property as you want others to treat yours.

Another component of treating other people with respect and consideration is treating their property as well as you treat your own.

This advice should not have to be stated or discussed, but personal experience proves it did in the past, does in the present, and will in the future because of the immutability of human nature.

The simplest example I've seen personally and in professional environments. People will take advantage of an individual or company who is buying them a meal. They will include more drinks, appetizers, substitutions, desserts, and after-dinner beverages than they would ever order when paying their own tab, thus taking advantage of the one who is treating them.

In the business world, I always coached employees upon their hiring to treat the company's money as if it were their own. Additionally, I would counsel them that their treatment of business funds would establish a reputation that would influence their requests for dollars for company activities and leadership advancement.

I could always recognize how they would behave within a few weeks of approving their employee expense reports.

Despite my instructions and warnings, some employees repeatedly took advantage of opportunities to overspend money. Almost all of them were amazed at my response, telling them they would not receive additional cash or options based on their behavior because I saw them act irresponsibly. They could not believe their actions would generate consequences.

Our actions will always reveal our respect for others' money and property. If we take advantage of someone else's money, we're almost sure to disrespect their property as well. Hall of Fame and legendary football coach Lou Holtz wisely advises us, "Do right. Do your best. Treat others as you want to be treated."

Establishing a reputation for respecting others' money and property enhances their trust in us, which may open untold doors of friendship, opportunity, and a richer life.

After all, don't others always want and expect us to respect their property?

If we all lived by The Golden Rule in the Bible and pronounced similarly in other cultures, we enjoy more peace. It says:

Luke 6:31

Do to others as you would have them do to you.

How This Lesson Applies to Me

____

____

____

____

30

Just because someone has something you don't have; it doesn't mean they are rich.

Perception is reality, as my late friend Bill "The Big Kahuna" Gardner said so often and appropriately.

It is incredible that despite education and experience, humans are prone to forming impressions based on illogical factors, stereotypes, and prejudices. I wager most of us have done it on occasion, some do it daily, and others will throughout their lifetime.

Sometimes our erroneous perceptions hurt us and other times, they hurt innocent people who are aware or unaware of our misguided actions.

An example of this hit me between the eyes during my real estate investment years, and it increased my sensitivity to prejudging others. I was a straight-commissioned sales rep who scrimped and saved every nickel to my name. A friend showed me the possibility of building a financial future free from debt and worry through real estate investing, and I took the risk, jumping into the market with both feet.

Every month was a nail-biter. I was always hoping rents would exceed expenses, and every surprise bill had to be paid with my meager savings.

One tenant asked me to put a screen door on her duplex unit so she could watch her grandson play in the driveway. I purchased one and hung it, very proud of the minor upgrade to the property.

When I returned to collect the next month's rent two weeks later, the door was damaged, and someone had torn out the screen. I was justifiably upset, but my lesson was just beginning.

When I asked my tenant what happened, she remarked her grandson and friends had destroyed the door, but without any empathy toward me. She expected me to pay to replace it immediately!

Her perception was that I was "rich" because I was her landlord. She believed every dollar of her rent was profit to me, and she didn't know nor did she care about my expenses or risks.

As the author, Harper Lee said, "People generally see what they look for and hear what they listen for." My argument that I was a struggling young business guy fighting to make ends meet fell on my tenant's deaf ears. To her, all that mattered was I was the landlord, and that meant I was rich.

James 3:14

But if you harbor bitter envy and selfish ambition in your hearts, do not boast about it or deny the truth.

How This Lesson Applies to Me

____

____

____

____

31

Even if they are rich, it is no excuse for abusing them or their property.

Yes, this closely aligns with number 29, but it is so vital it merits repeating.

There is no excuse for abusing or taking advantage of the property of others, whether they are rich, a large business, or a perceived privileged group, period.

If we shortsightedly take from others by depriving them of their property, we will eventually be discovered and penalized for our transgression. Regardless of the size of the act, we will suffer a loss of trust worth much more than any advantage or satisfaction we experienced from our ill-advised action.

Conversely, if we respect and handle others' property respectfully, trust in us will grow. People will trust us with more and more valuable possessions as we continue to prove trustworthy.

There are a handful of friends I would trust my daughter's life with because they repeatedly confirmed their honor over many years and instances.

Abraham Lincoln said, "Set an example of trustworthiness. People have confidence in trustworthy individuals. Whether you're seeking employees, customers, or both, a culture of integrity is priceless."

Dependability and consistency are critical components of a trustworthy individual as they increase others' trust in us.

But, fail once, and all of the faith we have built over time is destroyed. Furthermore, re-establishing trust is significantly more difficult after a fall because we don't start at the beginning but from a place of distrust. Depending on our actions, it may take years to reach the beginning, and we may never regain the level of trust others extended us.

Billy Graham was not only the premiere evangelist of the 20th century but was known as the pastor to the presidents, counseling twelve from Truman to Trump. It's hard to imagine anyone more upright or whose advice positively impacted people during that period. While Graham's trustworthiness stands above everyone, there are too many examples of believable individuals who forfeited their integrity with one or more missteps.

Bernie Madoff is a recent example of an investment tycoon trusted by wealthy and powerful people to handle and increase their assets' value. His reputation created a line of people wanting his attention and Midas' touch to prosper their future. He successfully perpetuated his scheme making his 2008 fall more astonishing, impoverishing more clients and damaging more people through the resulting ripple effect throughout the economy.

There is no excuse for abusing others' property, which will ruin our future like it did for Madoff. Following Graham's example will lead us to a healthier, happier, and more prosperous future financially and spiritually.

Luke 16:12

And if you have not been trustworthy with someone else's property, who will give you property of your own?

How This Lesson Applies to Me

32

Be patient. Nothing is free, and you have to pay dues to reap the rewards in life.

We naturally desire things to enjoy and improve our life's journey, and impatience about how "fast" that happens is also a common and instinctive trait.

Patience and deferred gratification are learned behaviors based on the principle that we have to prepare and work to earn the best rewards in life. Substantial achievements result when time and effort are applied and multiplied.

During my lifetime, I've witnessed the advancement of what some call the "fast-food society." Expectations for rapid and easy celebrity and success dominate society. "Influencers" who realize "fame" based on shaking their bottoms in 10-second videos are celebrated and enriched without contributing anything of substance, or value. They provide nothing that will withstand the test of time.

"We want what we want, and we want it now" is the demand from pop culture. Annual introductions of new cell phones with little advancements are anticipated and trumpeted more than breakthrough science or technologies that will impact people for generations.

It is easy to be swept into the frenzy of quick fame and fortune. Still, it is the better choice for everyone to maximize contributions over time to benefit the most significant number of people.

With scarce exceptions, we are all forgotten over time. The only question is: how quickly?

Rudolph Valentino was the heartthrob actor of his day, celebrated and envied by millions. He died at 31 in 1926 and is unknown to most people today. Do we hear of anyone citing his impact on their lives today? His meteoric ascent and flameout should be an example of the futility of worldly fame.

What is significantly more important is being able to look back on our lives and ask ourselves, *did we spend our lives creating, building, touching people, and or contributing to the benefit of future generations despite them never knowing us?*

Mother Teresa focused on helping others physically and spiritually, sacrificing her own opportunities for personal success. Among her efforts, she founded the Missions of Charity, which continues assisting the poorest of the poor long after her passing. She did not seek fame and did not use it for herself but employed it to expand the positive impact of her mission.

Which path should we choose for our journey?

Resist instant gratification. Resist the pursuit of fame without substance. Study, prepare, work, discover your mission, pay the price for experience, and deliver your impact on people today and beyond your lifetime. Doing so will enrich your life and earn heavenly rewards.

"Don't give up what you most want in life for something you think you want now." – Richard G. Scott

Colossians 1:11

being strengthened with all power according to his glorious might so that you may have great endurance and patience.

Psalms 103:16

...the wind blows over it and it is gone,
and its place remembers it no more.

How This Lesson Applies to Me

____

____

____

____

33

Most rich and successful people paid their dues. Learn from them, but don't envy them.

Our natural response to viewing rich and successful people is jealousy and envy. "*Why are they rich and not me?*" we think. We speculate the cause of their advantage. Did their family provide them with wealth? Did they take advantage of poor people to succeed? Every thought turns to ill-gotten gain because acknowledging that someone worked hard and earned their rewards threatens our self-esteem.

Yes, some people were blessed to be born on the one-yard line, and others climbed over innocents to achieve their prosperity. However, they are the exceptions and not worthy of our study.

More often than not, affluent and powerful individuals earned their gains the old-fashioned way. They worked hard for it. In addition, they all overcame one or more setbacks and many failures before achieving the not-so-instant overnight success.

Studying and emulating the character and habits of successful people is not only the American way but will almost be a guarantee to further our achievements.

President Abraham Lincoln is an outstanding example of one born of modest means, self-educated, and employing persistence to attain the highest office in the land. Before he was elected president in 1860, he failed many more times than he succeeded, including:

- 1832 Lost his job and was defeated for the state legislature.
- 1833 Failed in business.
- 1835 His sweetheart died.
- 1836 Had a nervous breakdown.
- 1838 Lost a race for Speaker of the House in Illinois.
- 1843 Lost a nomination for Congress.
- 1848 Lost a renomination for Congress after he won the election in 1846.
- 1849 Rejected for land officer.
- 1854 Defeated for U.S. Senate.
- 1857 Defeated for Vice-President nomination.
- 1858 Defeated for U.S. Senate.

President Calvin Coolidge's quote on persistence illustrates the essentialness of perseverance to produce triumph:

"Nothing in this world can take the place of persistence. Talent will not; nothing is more common than unsuccessful men with talent. Genius will not; unrewarded genius is almost a proverb. Education will not; the world is full of educated derelicts. Persistence and determination alone are omnipotent. The slogan 'Press On!' has solved and always will solve the problems of the human race."

Madam C.J. Walker is an amazing example of overcoming a disadvantaged birth and finding an American's path to success. Yes, like most of you, I was unaware of her accomplishments until later in life.

Madam Walker was an African-American and the first in her family born into freedom in 1867. She married at 14 to escape an abusive relative. Moving to St. Louis as a single mother at 21, she took in laundry, struggling to earn a dollar a day. Her dandruff and inability to find and afford a treatment led her to create a remedy.

Madam Walker began and built a cosmetics business offering beauty products for black women, making her the first self-made African-American woman millionaire in America. She shared her success with others through philanthropy and her leadership example.

Lincoln and Walker are but two of the innumerable examples of Americans worthy of our study who can inspire us to pursue our dreams.

James 3:16
For where you have envy and selfish ambition,
there you find disorder and every evil practice.

How This Lesson Applies to Me

____

____

____

____

34

Feelings of anger and envy don't hurt the other person half as much as they hurt you, because they prevent you from focusing and achieving positive results.

Believe it or not, the Austin, Texas, real estate market experienced a deep recession in the 1980s. It happened almost overnight after Congress passed a tax law that punished investors in the rental housing market.

I was a straight-commission sales rep who invested all my savings in rental housing during that period. The first few years went well, and I added to my portfolio almost annually. My plan to achieve financial independence was on track, and other investors and I never believed a market crash could occur. Then Congress acted.

First, my cash flow went negative to more than $ 2,500 a month as rents dropped, and it became difficult to find tenants. Renters delayed or stopped paying rent, damaged units, and left in the middle of the night owing me money. Buyers of my units reneged on their contracts necessitating foreclosures and reassuming ownership. Lenders, overwhelmed with investor defaults, only assisted the largest borrowers, which left me to fend for myself. One tenant compelled me to attempt collecting a week's rent at a time as I returned from my weekly business travel.

The pain, loss, and aggravation seemed to go on forever, and I didn't know if it would ever end.

Despite the adversity, I learned valuable life lessons. The most important was to forgive those who willingly, or unwillingly, abused my efforts to make the best of a bad situation for everyone.

I realized most of them were self-focused and didn't care or worry about my suffering. Any anger I might hold toward them didn't hurt them but inflicted stress on me, which affected my entire life.

Realizing my anger only hurt me made me realize that I could help myself by forgiving and forgetting my injuries, thus regaining my usual positive attitude to go forward with my life.

Almost immediately, life became more enjoyable, and my journey more prosperous.

The most important lesson I learned was this: Forgiving others is the greatest gift we can give ourselves because the inflictors of our pain don't usually care about us. How we respond to adversity is our choice. If we react in anger, our emotion controls us. We can move forward positively if we can forgive and let the anger go.

I've experienced many adversities since then, and this lesson consistently benefits my response.

Psalm 37:8
Refrain from anger and turn from wrath;
do not fret—it leads only to evil.

How This Lesson Applies to Me

____

____

____

____

35

Strive for excellence in ALL things.

Former coach of the Green Bay Packers and Hall of Fame member Vince Lombardi best captured the benefit of pursuing excellence. He said, "Gentlemen, we are going to relentlessly chase perfection, knowing full well we will not catch it because nothing is perfect. But we are going to relentlessly chase it because, in the process, we will catch excellence. I am not remotely interested in just being good."

Oh, if we followed Lombardi's creed all the time! Too often, for one reason or another, we take our foot off the gas and accept an effort less than all out on an endeavor we are pursuing.

The result puts a brake on our momentum and makes us languish in varying degrees of mediocrity, never achieving optimum performance in any area of life. Few of us are self-motivated, and fewer still haven't awakened to achievement beyond their dreams because they gave their everything in a monumental quest.

If we're fortunate, someone will care about us early in life and will inspire and motivate us to exert all of our energy all of the time in pursuit of our dreams.

Former Dallas Cowboys coach Tom Landry said, "Leadership is getting someone to do what they don't want to do to achieve what they want to achieve." Every athlete wants to win a championship, but very few will pay the price in preparation without coaches pushing them to do so.

The first time we achieve more than we dreamed because of an extraordinary effort, it opens our eyes to the possibilities of accomplishing more than we ever imagined.

When I led the Austin Junior Chamber of Commerce (Jaycees), we followed a year so successful that no one thought the group could achieve more. Thankfully, our members didn't rest on their laurels but chose to work even harder to help more community members. Our resulting impact was far beyond what any of us could have imagined.

Jim Davis's quote expressed our feelings when we looked back on our achievements that year. "It is amazing what you can do when you don't know what you can't do."

Achievement increases confidence, and confidence allows us to set and reach higher goals. Whether or not we reach those higher goals, we will almost always achieve more than our prior lower objectives.

Our choice every day is whether or not to give life our all. My biggest regrets were when I didn't wholeheartedly pursue worthy missions. The pain of my failures fueled growth and future success, and my victories exceeded my abilities and hopes, thanks to blessings from above.

Until our last breath, opportunities and choices present themselves to us daily. I hope each of us can reach our end satisfied; we gave our all and left nothing undone.

George Halas of the Chicago Bears (archrival to the Green Bay Packers) summed up giving our best effort always saying, "Nobody who ever gave their best regretted it."

Colossians 3:23

Whatever you do, work at it with all your heart,
as working for the Lord, not for human masters.

How This Lesson Applies to Me

____

____

____

____

36

To be an effective leader, you must also be a good follower.

People who need this the most will dismiss it as simple advice. They spend their time as followers, plotting to assume a leadership role. When their opportunity comes, they view themselves as superior to their followers and rule as the pharaohs of the past.

My experience affirms that the most outstanding leaders were also universally good followers. Cherished leaders learn why their peers are on the team.

From every experience they had as a follower, they can learn what motivates their teammates, when to push people for maximum contributions to the organization, where to discipline (privately) and reward (publicly) team members, and how to inspire individuals to achieve goals never visualized and impact people for generations to come.

The resulting wisdom for those who grasp it is: The most successful leaders are servant leaders who lead by example because of their experience as good followers.

Moses and Joshua are two great examples from the Bible for us to emulate. Most of us won't wait as long as they did for our opportunities to lead, but their experience is beneficial.

Moses was the adopted son of Pharoah in Egypt. Everyone expected him to ascend to the throne when his father crossed the river into eternity. After discovering his birthright and killing an Egyptian, he escaped into the desert. God spent 40 years preparing him to lead his people into the promised land as their foretold deliverer. He learned to follow God, and his inability to speak necessitated his continuing to follow God's will after his appointment. He was 80 years old when he led his people out of Egypt and led them for 40 more years.

Joshua was a chief lieutenant of Moses and served for the 40 years Moses led Israel. Loyalty, a servant's heart, and preparation to succeed Moses marked his tenure. Upon Moses' death, Joshua succeeded him and finally led Israel into the land of their promise. Again, Joshua experienced success when he continued to follow God's instruction and failed when he didn't seek and follow God's direction.

Moses and Joshua exhibited patience, loyalty, obedience, life-long learning, and leading by example with a servant's heart. If we learn from them and live accordingly, success and happiness will likely follow.

Joshua 1:5b - 6

As I was with Moses, so I will be with you; I will never leave you nor forsake you. Be strong and courageous, because you will lead these people to inherit the land I swore to their ancestors to give them.

How This Lesson Applies to Me

____

____

____

____

37

Be honest. ALWAYS tell the truth.

People will forgive a mistake but will never trust a liar.

While we don't always realize the benefit of being honest when it occurs, it will always benefit us long-term in everything.

Salespeople have a reputation for stretching the truth, which makes wise potential customers skeptical of their pitches. Savvy salespeople know the first thing they sell is themselves, and the first essential trait is truthfulness.

As a young, straight-commissioned sales rep, the first order I received from my largest customer arrived incorrectly. They potentially would provide about one-third of my annual income.

"What happened?" they asked. After reviewing the order, I replied, "I made a mistake, and we will correct it promptly." I resolved the issue as promised quickly and proceeded to sell and service the account over several years.

My customer bought everything I offered that would benefit them. One day when I earned an order where a competitor had a better offering, I asked, "Why did you buy from me when XYZ had a better product?"

Their reply cemented lessons learned previously and was beneficial to me for a lifetime. "Because when you made a mistake early on, you owned it and were honest with us. You have always spoken honestly with us." My reward for telling the truth was more significant than I deserved, but it was appreciated.

In addition to telling the truth, our actions must always back up our words, or the words will be meaningless. As Ralph Waldo Emerson said, "What you do speaks so loud that I cannot hear what you say."

Furthermore, our reputation is earned and reinforced with consistent openness and honest communication. One transgression will cripple our future, destroying it for a lifetime. This is why building trust with people is the most important cornerstone for building relationships.

Without trust founded on truth, our dreams will remain ever elusive.

Ephesians 4:25
Therefore each of you must put off falsehood
and speak truthfully to your neighbor,
for we are all members of one body.

How This Lesson Applies to Me

____

____

____

____

38

WHAT YOU THINK IS WHAT YOU FEEL. THINK POSITIVE!

Despite the massive evidence and examples to the contrary over time in memorial, it is incredible how easy it is for people to develop negative attitudes about almost everything.

Find anyone who has achieved anything and you will find that they began their endeavor with a positive attitude. Additionally, virtually everyone who has earned success has overcome one or more failures, obstacles, and adverse experiences.

President Theodore Roosevelt overcame health issues, and the deaths of his mother and first wife on the same day, to achieve outstanding accomplishments as an outdoorsman, a military leader, and as the president of the United States.

He knew his attitude would lead to his feelings, and his ability to overcome adversity was a requirement to achieve his ambitions. He fearlessly pursued the highest dreams proving his philosophy, "Believe you can, and you're halfway there." His example inspires people to persevere through difficult times and never give up on their aspirations.

Charles Lindbergh is remembered as the first pilot to fly solo across the Atlantic in 1927. Before his attempt, five pilots perished attempting the same feat while pursuing the Orteig prize of $25,000. Lindbergh's positive attitude influenced his courage which led to his success.

It is inconceivable that anyone would attempt achievements like Lindbergh's, the Lewis and Clark expedition, the manned space flight to the moon, Columbus's discovery of America, or any other grand accomplishment without a positive attitude toward the effort.

Lindbergh said, "Success is not measured by what a man accomplishes, but by the opposition he has encountered and the courage with which he has maintained the struggle against overwhelming odds." Opposition is not limited to other people, but the world we live in also.

Lindbergh's success prepared him for the horrific kidnapping and murder of his first son in 1932. Like all humans, he was imperfect, but worthy of our admiration for his flying achievements.

Everyone I've known with a negative attitude lives a seemingly miserable life devoid of achievement. They are unworthy of emulation or association and rarely attract anyone into their orbit.

The most important lesson I've learned is, *you can't do anything positive with a negative attitude.*

Proverbs 23:7 – (KJV)
For as he thinketh in his heart, so is he.

How This Lesson Applies to Me

____

____

____

____

39

Revere the past. The wisdom of the ages is at your fingertips.

When I first wrote the words above, no one disputed them; many would feel the advice was unnecessary. But, as we passed the 2020 threshold, attacks on past societies, especially Western civilization and Caucasians, increased in number and intensity.

People who have never achieved any personal accomplishments criticize and erase (*Canceled* is the term used today.) the grand achievements of individuals because of as little as a person's one offense against today's society, regardless of its perception during the offender's lifetime. What foolishness!

We know good and bad people and events, they are just a keystroke away with available technology. The opportunity to learn from others' mistakes has benefitted all societies over time, yet we have people who want to ignore all history and experience each day without its advantage.

An additional argument against history is that people have evolved, and still are, so past societal norms and laws don't apply to people today. If human nature evolved as they advocate, their point would merit consideration.

My argument is human nature has not, is not, and will not evolve. Therefore, from the beginning, all human experience is beneficial for us. Our responsibility is to learn from the past, grow and live in the present, and give our descendants a better future than what has blessed us.

Thucydides, an Athenian general and historian, said around 400 years BC, "Human nature is the one constant through human history. It is always there."

The most evident proof exists early in the Bible when Adam and Eve disobey God in Genesis 3. When God catches them and asks why they dishonored him, Adam pointed his finger at Eve and blamed her. Not to be outdone, Eve pointed her finger at the serpent and accused him.

We see the exact natural response today in young children. When something breaks and a parent asks a group of children what happened, their unanimous answer is, "I didn't do it!" or, "It's not my fault." Nothing has changed over the millennia! Taking responsibility for our actions is a learned discipline.

H.P. Blavatsky was a 19th-century author and philosopher. She said, "Civilization may progress, human nature will remain the same throughout the ages."

The constancy of human nature not only means we can learn from our predecessors but also confidently interact with people during our lives, understanding their behavior.

Learn early, learn often, never quit learning, but continue gaining knowledge and wisdom for a lifetime. As Ecclesiastes 1:9 says, "What has been will be again, what has been done will be done again; there is nothing new under the sun."

Time and people past stand ready to serve us today, if we're wise enough to receive their gift.

Proverbs 19:8

The one who gets wisdom loves life; the one
who cherishes understanding will soon prosper.

How This Lesson Applies to Me

40

There are two types of people. Those who look for ways to make things happen, and those who look for reasons why things can't happen. They both achieve what they see.

I didn't notice this phenomenon in school (hopefully not because of poor observation skills but because I wasn't applying myself). However, it was apparent everywhere once I entered the real work world and exerted myself.

Everyone fits into one of these two categories in most of their behavior. I'm not judging anyone; we all are free to live as we choose. Pointing this truth out is more of an alert to observe and realize how individuals function so we can maximize the achievement of our goals and dreams.

If we're satisfied where we are, this subject is unimportant. If we have aspirations to achieve more and be more than we are today, it is a crucial principle to aid our efforts to be the best we can be.

Similar to associating with negative people who will only influence our attitude negatively, people who look for reasons not to act and make things happen will always disappoint us. They have an endless arsenal of excuses for why they can't accomplish their responsibilities or requests from others.

Actor Tyrese Gibson said, "Excuses sound best to the person that's making 'em up." He is correct because people who offer excuses become so used to doing so that they begin and become trapped into always offering them even when one isn't necessary. They also become oblivious to the realization that their excuses are so obvious almost everyone sees them for what they are, a weak rationalization.

***

The second category of people is those who make things happen. Their inspirational stories of overcoming adversity, intermittent failure, obstacles to attaining their dreams, and sometimes monumental success, are worthy of our study and emulation. The motivational speaker Jim Rohn says, "If you really want to do something, you'll find a way. If you don't, you'll find an excuse."

William M. Winans, a Methodist minister in the early 1900s, said, "Not doing more than the average is what keeps the average down." In other words, we should always strive to do our best and exceed our team's average to contribute to its success rather than drag it into mediocrity by accepting an ordinary performance.

I've told teams there are three steps in achieving our personal goals and team objectives. They are I can; I will, I did.

First, we must believe we can achieve our goal and contribute our share, voicing our confidence with *I can!*

Second, we must act with the commitment of *I will!* We do not wait for perfect information or timing but move forward at the appropriate time, relentlessly overcoming all setbacks and roadblocks until we celebrate our achievements.

Third, we bask in our accomplishment, saying *I did!* While the exhilaration of success is a wonderful reward, we accrue other benefits. Every victory increases our capabilities and confidence for further achievement. There is no greater feeling than saying "I did it!" after achieving an objective.

***

The Apollo 13 mission to the moon in 1970 is famous for NASA overcoming many technological challenges to return three astronauts safely to Earth. The 1995 movie of the same name enabled the audience to experience a small fraction of the stress everyone associated with the journey lived.

Chief Flight Director Gene Kranz's positive CAN-do spirit pushed the crisis-laden team beyond what they believed they could achieve. His creed, "Failure is not an option," infected everyone to maximize their individual performance and execute their team duties setting aside self-interests.

Working together, they created a replacement part from non-essential pieces available on the aircraft. They then instructed the astronauts step-by-step on how to replicate the feat on their ship before their oxygen expired. Success averted catastrophe and death and enabled a triumphant return to home.

Their example is an outstanding model for us to follow.

***

If we want to enjoy our life to the fullest, we should always look for ways to get things done, and only associate with others who think likewise. If we do so, we'll accomplish more, positively impact many more people, and set a better example for those who follow us.

Hebrews 11:1

Now faith is confidence in what we hope
for and assurance about what we do not see.

How This Lesson Applies to Me

41

Former coach of the Carolina Panthers, Dom Capers has a great philosophy. It is:
Expect Nothing!
Work Hard!
Prepare for the worst!
Hope for the best!

What a great philosophy of life!

As we discussed in 26, no matter how good another person is, we all let others down periodically. No one wants or plans to do it, but we will inevitably fail others.

The closer we are to a person, and the higher our expectations, the more crushing the disappointment that they, like us, are merely human. Our proper response is forgiveness, just as we hope for mercy when we let down others. Compassion from each party to the other person is essential to maintain and deepen any relationship.

Too often, people expect things to be given to them with little or no effort. The prosperity of our society softens us to the hardness of life. Observing undeserving people prosper through false fame and little effort leads us to seek the easy way out of work. But time in memorial proves hard work is the best and only path to long-term success.

Once again, easy times create a false sense of security that it will always be this good. While others play, we should prepare for tough times. If they come, we will endure and overcome them better than those who failed to prepare for difficulty. If adversity delays, we can enjoy life knowing we're ready for when the suffering appears.

Hope! It is one of the three essential attitudes of life, along with faith and love. Where we place, our Hope is as important as Hope itself. Faith in God and our eternal destination with Him provides us with an unshakeable foundation. Properly prepared for adversity, we can live confidently with a positive attitude of hope, knowing that regardless of the vagaries of life and the unknown path of our journey, we will conclude our travel in a safe harbor.

Jeremiah 29:11

"For I know the plans I have for you," declares the Lord, "plans to prosper you and not to harm you, plans to give you hope and a future."

How This Lesson Applies to Me

____

____

____

____

42

Be creative. Always be thinking of ways to improve yourself and/or the things you're doing.

One of the greatest blessings in life is our opportunity to grow, discover, learn, and become better people. Where we begin and the steps we take along the way don't dictate the entire journey but do contribute experience.

Every day, we have the freedom to modify the direction of our path or choose a new approach. All along the way, we should acknowledge others' efforts in laying the foundation of our experience and serving our community.

I love to evaluate every episode in life for lessons, good and bad, to help me better encounter the future. Looking back at events like coaches reviewing the game film to better prepare for the next contest stimulates ideas to make better decisions, helps me avoid making the same mistake again, and arouses suggestions I never thought of previously.

Thinking of ideas without prejudice to others' prior attempts or comments often provides me with my most successful achievements.

Creativity is in our nature. As the Chinese artist Al Weiwei said, "Creativity is part of human nature. It can only be untaught." The most creative people are young children because they have not failed or received rejection of their dreams and ideas. Their vivid imaginations explore regions of creativity virtually extinct in adult brains.

Discouragement, ridicule, and failure have disabled more people than all the wars in the history of the world. But we are never defeated as long as we think, create, and do. Only quitting our effort sentences us to live the remainder of our lives stuck where we are.

Obstacles are no reason to quit. Nelson Mandela, who overcame many obstacles to lead his country, said, "It always seems impossible until it's done."

David Marshall "Carbine" Williams found himself in prison in the early 1900s for killing a man. Thinking of ideas to improve firearms enabled him to survive thirty days in "the hole" when previously no one had lasted more than 7 days. Overcoming strong resistance and precedent, he invented an improvement for the M-1 carbine in prison, which saved untold numbers of Allied soldiers in World War II. His continued efforts upon leaving prison resulted in him receiving more than 50 patents. His creativity served his life and the world.

If we're going to achieve all we can in life, we must continue to breath's end. Achieving goals, setting new objectives, pressing the envelope, leaving our comfort zone, and always thinking of new ideas will sweeten our journey, help us repay our forebearers, and bless those who come behind us. Author Jack Canfield said, "If we're not a little bit uncomfortable every day, we're not growing. All the good stuff is outside our comfort zone."

Be creative every day! Live life as an adventure, not a sentence! We never know where it may lead us!

1 Thessalonians 1:3

We remember before our God and Father your work
produced by faith, your labor prompted by love, and your
endurance inspired by hope in our Lord Jesus Christ.

How This Lesson Applies to Me

43

Make friends with as many people as possible.

Friendships are the most important thing in life next to your relationship with God and your family. If you have friends and you are a true friend in return, you will be able to have a wide range of opportunities during your life.

Starting in life, we tend to focus on the present and rarely consider the influence of today on the future. After time passes, it is easier to see how our past dictates our present and sets the stage for our future.

If we're fortunate, by accident or understanding, we have treated others well and forged many friendships. Our tomorrows will arise full of opportunity, and friends will stand ready to assist us as we pursue our dreams.

If we are short-sighted and self-centered, our friend cupboard will be bare, and our destiny will appear limited. If we continue to chase our hopes, we'll have few willing to help us, and our objectives will seem daunting.

To have friends, we must first be a friend. True friends are genuine, authentic, considerate, loyal, and trustworthy. They naturally possess loving servant hearts, always wanting to help others.

Walter Winchell, a renowned journalist in the middle of the 20th century said, "A friend is one who walks in when others walk out." There are few joys greater than knowing our friends will stand tall with us when trouble arrives, instead of running for the high grass to avoid inconvenience. These are true friends with servant's hearts.

The centuries-old popular proverb, "A friend in need is a friend indeed" encourages us to live serving others.

My late friend, Alan Goldsberry, would never fail to ask me when we communicated, "What can I do to help you today?" It was a great question, which we should emulate relentlessly, and he served as a great example.

We must be vigilant for insincere, inauthentic people who will only help us when it is convenient for them and always look for the first opportunity to leverage their help for a return service. At the first sign of them, we should politely decline their offers and avoid a relationship with them.

In the movie, *It's a Wonderful Life*, George Bailey thought he wasted his life from a materialistic view. He finally learned he was the richest man in town because he made so many friends over a lifetime.

If we live the characteristics of a true friend like George Bailey, the blessing of bountiful relationships will enrich our lives here and beyond.

Proverbs 18:24

One who has unreliable friends soon comes to ruin,
but there is a friend who sticks closer than a brother.

How This Lesson Applies to Me

____

____

____

____

A Surprise Present

"Your spiritual gifts were not given for your own benefit but for the benefit of others, just as other people were given gifts for your benefit."

—Rick Warren

A Touch from Heaven and Extension of Impact

I'm blessed to share the story of my son John's brief life and passing to help others experiencing loss in their lives. It is bitter, as I wish he were still on this earth, but sweet that he continues to impact others positively beyond his lifetime.

I've encountered many people who have benefitted from John's story, but none more touching than this one.

***

The week before Father's Day 2022, Burke Allen, my expert media rep, created a radio and television pitch around the story and the letter I wrote to John when he was six months old. I had multiple opportunities to present it in four to ninety-minute segments. I often discuss subjects with the media and never know if anything I say assists anyone.

A four-minute segment at 7:39 a.m. was booked with Doug Wagner on WMT in Cedar Rapids, Iowa Thursday, June 16th. I've been privileged to appear with Doug several times, and he conducts the brief interviews very efficiently and always makes me look good.

I also had an appointment to drop my truck off at the dealership for service at 7:00 a.m. that morning. I planned to appear for the interview in the service department lounge. As the time approached 7:35 a.m., I decided to move to the sales lounge as the service lounge was too busy and loud.

The sales lounge was perfect as no one was there, and it was too early for much sales activity. I completed my set-up for the interview, the phone rang, and Doug prepared me to go on-air.

Going live, Doug directed our conversation, asking me about John's life and passing, the letter, and what I learned that could help others experiencing grief for any loss.

As I spoke to Doug, I noticed a man open the door, come through the lounge, and leave my eyesight, but I didn't pay much attention to him. Shortly after that, the four minutes were over, and Doug and I said our goodbyes.

Thankfully, my truck was ready, and I left the dealership for the hour drive home. That morning, I began listening to *An American Life* audiobook version. It is an autobiography of President Ronald Reagan, and he read the audio version.

I was just at the point where President Reagan detailed how seemingly small insignificant things often provided life-changing impacts. He recalled his experience breaking into the radio business. Reagan experienced rejection, failure, firing, changes in management, and other setbacks before his big break appeared. He testified that every obstacle and adversity contributed to his monumental success in life.

Just then, my phone rang from a number I didn't recognize. At the next red light, I noticed the voicemail was from a man at the dealership. *Oh no,* I thought. *There must be a problem with my truck or the transaction.*

***

I reluctantly returned the call. The man asked me if I was the person who had recently spoken on the phone in the sales lounge, and I acknowledged it was I.

His following statement shook me and humbled my heart. "Thank you for what you said on the phone. I recently lost a daughter and prayed to God last night to send someone who could comfort me, and I believe He sent you at this specific time to do so."

Wow! My first instinct was *this was definitely a God moment!* Before I fully processed the ramifications of what just happened, my attention turned to availing myself to helping this man in the depth of his grief.

I offered my deepest condolences and stated I was and will be available for him and his family in any way at any time that may benefit them. I shared some of the lessons I learned and the story of how I came to write *Surviving Grief by God's Grace.*

He appreciated my time and comments, and I could sense his desperate search for relief because I had walked that path. I did not ask him what happened to his beautiful daughter because it did not make any difference to me or my serving him. I did not tell him I understood what he was going through because I feel every loss is different, just as everyone grieves individually. I tell people I have an idea of what they're going through, but I understand and respect the uniqueness of every situation.

After our five-or-six-minute call, we offered blessings to each other, and the call ended. As I continued my return home, a variety of thoughts flooded my mind. *What just happened?*

***

I don't believe in coincidences and the odds that the number of individual events that occurred precisely at the right time to produce this moment is astronomically high.

No, this was God's will and purpose of utilizing so many components to achieve what some may believe to be a small outcome:

- Burke Allen's idea for a Father's Day interview pitch set the stage.

- Doug Wagner liked the pitch and booked me to appear with him.
- Multiple factors orchestrated my timing to be at the dealership that morning.
- Several individuals arrived at the service lounge at the same time.
- The service lounge congestion prompted me to retreat to the sales lounge.
- The man walked through the lounge, listened to enough of the four-minute interview to be blessed, asked for my number from the service department, and called me.

My experience of losing John, accepting the interview booking, moving to the sales lounge, responding to Doug's questions on-air since the man could only hear my end of the interview, and my phone call with the man were all directed by God's hand.

***

The more I thought about it, the more grateful and humble it made me. God utilized all of these people and platforms, including John's story and mine, to comfort this man and his family.

Many believe God is too busy with the big things in the world to care for or become involved with the small day-to-day items in our lives. This incident is another example of God being with us constantly, using us for His purposes when we follow His will and demonstrate to others His love for us.

Philippians 4:6-7 - comforted me in my darkest days. It says, "Do not be anxious about anything, but in every situation, by prayer and petition, with thanksgiving, present your requests to God. And the peace of God, which transcends all understanding, will guard your hearts and your minds in Christ Jesus."

It proves He is there for us, loves us, and wants us to live in peace, and have hope for the future.

***

I hope that man and his family seek God for comfort and healing. I would be honored to avail myself to help them in any way.

And I pray this story and example of God's presence, love, and provision will bless you.

Finally, my earnest desire is to live looking for God in the minute events of my life. Looking for Him in everything enriches our days and service to Him. I hope you will also.

Future Presents

"The clock is running. Make the most of today. Time waits for no man. Yesterday is history. Tomorrow is a mystery. Today is a gift. That is why it is called the present." – Alice Morse Earle

Afterword

John's passing stopped time for us. Slowly it resumed at glacial speed as we endured the previously unimaginable grief.

The shock of our loss shattered our hope for the future. Fortunately, a dinner with Buddy and Ginny Jones, who also lost a son, relit the spark of desire to live for the future.

Elizabeth's birth ten months later and the necessities of daily life salved our grief as it relentlessly advanced regardless of our feelings.

Writing *Surviving Grief by God's Grace* was more therapeutic for my healing process than I imagined. It began as my journal notes, which I shared with another family at church who lost their son five months after John passed. Their encouragement to share it with others transformed it from my daily notes to a published work for others benefit.

Now 25 years after my original letter to John and his passing, the book and my speaking efforts honor him and add impact to his too-short life. I'm honored more often than I dreamed when people communicate their appreciation for sharing John's story and my experience.

The principles I wrote for John's benefit in the event of my inability to teach him personally are as essential for a bountiful life today as when I wrote them. I hope reading them today will provide you and your family with multi-generational benefits.

Every day people suffer the loss of loved ones and grasp for comfort and a renewed hope of life in the future. My loss put me on the path earlier than some, and I desire *that Surviving Grief by God's Grace* may also benefit you in your most profound need.

I appreciate the lessons I learned from John's loss and the opportunities I have had to share them with others. John has impacted many more people beyond his lifetime than I could ever imagine. While I value the education from his passing, I would have preferred remaining ignorant and having him with me today. Too often, our choice isn't what we experience but how we respond to the event. I hope my response is worthy of John's price for my knowledge.

John's life was and is a present I benefit from every day. He left us, leaving my letter unopened and unread, and he only experienced too few present days.

My hope and mission in sharing the letter and additional context is you will open the present, benefit from it, and improve others' lives during your many present days.

THE GATE OF THE YEAR

'God Knows'

And I said to the man who stood at the gate of the year:

"Give me a light that I may tread safely into the unknown."

And he replied:

"Go out into the darkness and put your hand into the Hand of God.

That shall be to you better than light and safer than a known way."

So I went forth, and finding the Hand of God, trod gladly into the night.

And He led me towards the hills and the breaking of day in the lone East.

Excerpted from 'God Knows' by Minnie Louise Haskins, published 1912. The popular name of the poem is *The Gate of the Year.*

Bibliography

Battle, Richard V., *Navigating Life's Journey: Common Sense in Uncommon Times*, Denver, Outskirts Press, 2020.

Battle, Richard V., *Surviving Grief by God's Grace*, Bloomington, Authorhouse, 2002.

www.Biblegateway.com.

Covey, Stephen R., *The 7 Habits of Highly Effective People*, New York, Fireside, 1989.

www.Dictionary.com.

Frankl, Viktor, *Man's Search for Meaning*, New York, Touchstone Press, 1959.

www.Merriam-webster.com.

Portis, Charles, *True Grit*, New York, Simon & Schuster, 1968.

https://www.primidi.com/david_marshall_williams/legacy.

Reagan, Ronald, *An American Life*, New York, Simon & Schuster, 1990.

https://en.wikipedia.org/wiki/The_Gate_of_the_Year.

Appendix – A
Scriptures

Designates lesson scripture appeared. (11)
NIV unless denoted.

- Genesis 1:27 - So God created mankind in his own image, in the image of God he created them; male and female he created them. (18)
- Exodus 20:12 – Honor your father and your mother, so that you may live long in the land the Lord your God is giving you. (2)
- Joshua 1:5b - 6 - As I was with Moses, so I will be with you; I will never leave you nor forsake you. Be strong and courageous, because you will lead these people to inherit the land I swore to their ancestors to give them. (36)
- Job 8:21 -He will yet fill your mouth with laughter and your lips with shouts of joy. (20)
- Psalm 37:8 - Refrain from anger and turn from wrath; do not fret—it leads only to evil.(34)
- Psalms 103:16 - the wind blows over it and it is gone, and its place remembers it no more. (32)
- Psalm 119:71 - It was good for me to be afflicted so that I might learn your decrees. (4)
- Proverbs 1:7 - The fear of the LORD is the beginning of knowledge, but fools despise wisdom and instruction. (17)

- Proverbs 11:7 - Hopes placed in mortals die with them; all the promise of their power comes to nothing. (26)
- Proverbs 12:26 - The righteous choose their friends carefully, but the way of the wicked leads them astray. (16)
- Proverbs 23:7 – (KJV), For as he thinketh in his heart, so is he. (38)
- Proverbs 14:7 - Stay away from a fool, for you will not find knowledge on their lips. (7)
- Proverbs 14:17 - A quick-tempered person does foolish things, and the one who devises evil schemes is hated. (22)
- Proverbs 14:23 - All hard work brings a profit, but mere talk leads only to poverty. (21)
- Proverbs 15:4 - The soothing tongue is a tree of life, but a perverse tongue crushes the spirit. (6)
- Proverbs 17:17 - A friend loves at all times, and a brother is born for a time of adversity. (27)
- Proverbs 18:15 - The heart of the discerning acquires knowledge, for the ears of the wise seek it out. (3)
- Proverbs 18:24 - One who has unreliable friends soon comes to ruin, but there is a friend who sticks closer than a brother. (43)
- Proverbs 19:8 - The one who gets wisdom loves life; the one who cherishes understanding will soon prosper. (39)
- Proverbs 21:2 - A person may think their own ways are right, but the Lord weighs the heart. (23)
- Proverbs 22:3 - The prudent see danger and take refuge, but the simple keep going and pay the penalty. (24)
- Ecclesiastes 1:9 - What has been will be again, what has been done will be done again; there is nothing new under the sun. (39)

- Isaiah 40:31 says, But those who hope in the Lord will renew their strength. They will soar on wings like eagles; they will run and not grow weary; they will walk and not be faint. (1)
- Isaiah 41:10 - So do not fear, for I am with you; do not be dismayed, for I am your God. I will strengthen you and help you; I will uphold you with my righteous right hand. (14)
- Jeremiah 29:11 - For I know the plans I have for you," declares the Lord, "plans to prosper you and not to harm you, plans to give you hope and a future." (41)
- Matthew 7:12 - So in everything, do to others what you would have them do to you, for this sums up the Law and the Prophets. (28)
- Matthew 23:12 - For those who exalt themselves will be humbled, and those who humble themselves will be exalted. (11)
- Mark 9:23 – "'If you can?'" said Jesus. "Everything is possible for one who believes." (15)
- Luke 6:31 - Do to others as you would have them do to you. (29)
- Luke 16:12 - And if you have not been trustworthy with someone else's property, who will give you property of your own? (31)
- Romans 6:21 - What benefit did you reap at that time from the things you are now ashamed of? Those things result in death! (25)
- Romans 12:10 - Be devoted to one another in love. Honor one another above yourselves. (27)
- Romans 13:7 - Give to everyone what you owe them: If you owe taxes, pay taxes; if revenue, then revenue; if respect, then respect; if honor, then honor. (10)
- 1 Corinthians 4:2 - Now it is required that those who have been given a trust must prove faithful. (12)

- Ephesians 4:25 - Therefore each of you must put off falsehood and speak truthfully to your neighbor, for we are all members of one body. (37)
- Philippians 4:6-7 - comforted me in my darkest days. It says, "Do not be anxious about anything, but in every situation, by prayer and petition, with thanksgiving, present your requests to God. And the peace of God, which transcends all understanding, will guard your hearts and your minds in Christ Jesus." (A Touch from Heaven and Extension of Impact)
- Philippians 4:8 - Finally, brothers and sisters, whatever is true, whatever is noble, whatever is right, whatever is pure, whatever is lovely, whatever is admirable—if anything is excellent or praiseworthy—think about such things. (5)
- Philippians 4:12-13 - I know what it is to be in need, and I know what it is to have plenty. I have learned the secret of being content in any and every situation, whether well fed or hungry, whether living in plenty or in want. I can do all this through him who gives me strength. (19)
- Colossians 1:11 - being strengthened with all power according to his glorious might so that you may have great endurance and patience. (32)
- Colossians 2: 6b-7 - ...continue to live your lives in him, rooted and built up in him, strengthened in the faith as you were taught, and overflowing with thankfulness. (19)
- Colossians 3:23 - Whatever you do, work at it with all your heart, as working for the Lord, not for human masters. (35)
- 1 Thessalonians 1:3 - We remember before our God and Father your work produced by faith, your labor

prompted by love, and your endurance inspired by hope in our Lord Jesus Christ. (42)

- 1 Thessalonians 5:18 - Give thanks in all circumstances; for this is God's will for you in Christ Jesus. (8)
- Hebrews 11:1 - Now faith is confidence in what we hope for and assurance about what we do not see. (40)
- Hebrews 11:6 – And without faith it is impossible to please God, because anyone who comes to him must believe that he exists and that he rewards those who earnestly seek him. (1)
- James 3:5 (TLB) sums it up: The tongue is a small thing, but what enormous damage it can do. (6)
- James 3:14 – But if you harbor bitter envy and selfish ambition in your hearts, do not boast about it or deny the truth. (30)
- James 3:16 – For where you have envy and selfish ambition, there you find disorder and every evil practice. (33)
- James 3:17 – But the wisdom that comes from heaven is first of all pure; then peace-loving, considerate, submissive, full of mercy and good fruit, impartial and sincere. (9)
- 1 John 3:18 - Dear children, let us not love with words or speech but with actions and in truth. (13)

Appendix B
Quotations

Designates lessons where quote appeared (23)

- Aesop - "After all is said and done, more is said than done." (12)
- Anonymous - "Every day's a perfect gift of time for us to use. Hours waiting to be filled in any way we choose. Each morning brings a quiet hope that rises with the sun. Each evening brings the sweet content that comes with work well done." (The Letter)
- Bill Battle - "Can't never did anything." (15)
- H.P. Blavatsky - "Civilization may progress, human nature will remain the same throughout the ages." (39)
- Richard Branson - "Please be polite. Nothing in life should erode the habit of saying thank you to people or praising them." (8)
- Kenneth Burke - "If decisions were a choice between alternatives, decisions would come easy. Decision is the selection and formulation of alternatives." (16)
- Jack Canfield - "If we're not a little bit uncomfortable every day, we're not growing. All the good stuff is outside our comfort zone." (42)
- Dom Capers, former Carolina football coach - "Expect nothing, Work Hard, Prepare for the worst, hope for the best." (41)

- Winston Churchill - “In War: Resolution. In Defeat: Defiance. In Victory: Magnanimity. In Peace: Good Will.” (11)
- Jerry Clower - “It’s obvious you’ve been educated beyond your intelligence.” (17)
- President Calvin Coolidge - “Nothing in this world can take the place of persistence. Talent will not; nothing is more common than unsuccessful men with talent. Genius will not; unrewarded genius is almost a proverb. Education will not; the world is full of educated derelicts. Persistence and determination alone are omnipotent. The slogan ‘Press On!’ has solved and always will solve the problems of the human race.” (33)
- Davy Crockett - “Be sure you’re right, then go ahead.” (23)
- Jim Davis - “It is amazing what you can do when you don’t know what you can’t do.” (35)
- Alice Morse Earle - “The clock is running. Make the most of today. Time waits for no man. Yesterday is history. Tomorrow is a mystery. Today is a gift. That is why it is called the present.” (Future Presents)
- Thomas Edison - “I have not failed. I just found 10,000 ways that didn’t work.” (13)
- Albert Einstein - “Stay away from negative people. They have a problem for every solution.” (7)
- Ralph Waldo Emerson - “The mind, once stretched by a new idea, never returns to its original dimensions.” (3)
- Ralph Waldo Emerson – “What you do speaks so loud that I cannot hear what you say.” (37)
- Henry Ford - “Think you can, or think you can’t. Either way, you’ll be right.” (5)
- Benjamin Franklin - “A friend in need is a friend indeed.” (27)

- Benjamin Franklin - "When you're good to others, you're best to yourselves." (28)
- Bill (The Big Kahuna) Gardner - "Perception is reality." (30)
- Tyrese Gibson - "Excuses sound best to the person that's making 'em up." (40)
- Chris Guillebeau - "If plan A fails, remember there are 25 more letters." (16)
- George Halas - "Nobody who ever gave their best regretted it." (35)
- Audrey Hepburn - "You can tell more about what a person says about others than what others say about him." (6)
- Lou Holtz - "Do right. Do your best. Treat others as you want to be treated." (29)
- Michael Hyatt - "You can't fail if you don't quit. You can't succeed if you don't start." (15)
- Robert T. Kiyosaki - "The reason so many people fail to achieve success is because they fail to fail enough times." (14)
- Gene Kranz - "Failure is not an option." (40)
- Tom Landry - "Leadership is getting someone to do what they don't want to do to achieve what they want to achieve." (35)
- Harper Lee - "People generally see what they look for and hear what they listen for." (30)
- President Abraham Lincoln - "Set an example of trustworthiness. People have confidence in trustworthy individuals. Whether you're seeking employees, customers, or both, a culture of integrity is priceless." (31)

- Charles Lindbergh - "Success is not measured by what a man accomplishes, but by the opposition he has encountered and the courage with which he has maintained the struggle against overwhelming odds." (38)
- Vince Lombardi - "Gentlemen, we are going to relentlessly chase perfection, knowing full well we will not catch it because nothing is perfect. But we are going to relentlessly chase it because, in the process, we will catch excellence. I am not remotely interested in just being good." (35)
- Nelson Mandela - "It always seems impossible until it's done." (42)
- Rob Nalley – "Better never than late." (10)
- Old cowboy saying - "There has never been a horse that can't be rode, and there's never been a rider who can't be throwed." (11)
- Norman Vincent Peale - "You must feed your mind even as you feed your body, and to make your mind healthy, you must feed it nourishing wholesome thoughts." (7)
- Jim Rohn - "If you really want to do something you'll find a way. If you don't, you'll find an excuse." (40)
- Eleanor Roosevelt - "Life is not about expecting, hoping and wishing. It's about doing, being and becoming. It's about learning from the mistakes of others. You can't live long enough to make them all yourself." (The Lessons Opened)
- President Theodore Roosevelt - "Believe you can, and you're halfway there." (38)
- Richard G. Scott – "Don't give up what you most want in life for something you think you want now." (32)
- Hyrum W. Smith - "To reach any goal, you must leave your comfort zone." (13)

- Thucydides - "Human nature is the one constant through human history. It is always there." (39)
- Rick Warren - "Your spiritual gifts were not given for your own benefit but for the benefit of others, just as other people were given gifts for your benefit." (A surprise present)
- Al Weiwei - "Creativity is part of human nature. It can only be untaught." (42)
- William M. Winans - "Not doing more than the average is what keeps the average down" (40)
- Walter Winchell - "A friend is one who walks in when others walk out." (43)
- John Wooden - "Consider the rights of others before your own feelings, and the feelings of others before your own rights." (28)
- Zig Ziglar – "You can get everything you want in life by helping enough other people get what they want." (28)

Appendix C
Battle's Bullets

Designates lessons where bullet appeared (23)

- Nothing positive is ever accomplished with a negative attitude. (5)
- It is imperative to pursue every endeavor to success or failure. Doing so will lead us to greater heights of performance, and our setbacks will provide us with the seeds for success in other enterprises. (15)
- The easy way out is usually only easy in the short run. (22)
- The first time we achieve more than we dreamed because of an extraordinary effort, it opens our eyes to the possibilities of accomplishing more than our current dreams. (35)
- Achievement increases confidence in setting and reaching higher goals. Whether or not we reach those higher goals, we will almost always achieve more than our prior lower objectives. (35)
- I can, I will, I did. (12 and 40)
- I did is better than I will. (12)
- I'm on an unknown path to a known destiny.
- I've never had a bad experience saying "Thank You" (8)
- If we lengthen our perspective before faced with difficult circumstances, we're more likely to choose better paths leading to happier and more successful lives for us and those who follow us. (21)

- Forgiving others is the greatest gift we can give ourselves because the inflictors of our pain don't usually care about us. (34)
- Without trust founded on truth, our dreams will remain ever elusive. (37)
- Our responsibility is to learn from the past, grow and live in the present, and give our descendants a better future than blessed us. (39)
- Time in memorial proves hard work is the best and only path to long-term success. (41)
- We are never defeated as long as we think, create, and do. (42)
- If we're going to achieve all we can in life, we must continue to breath's end. (42)
- Smart people learn from their experience. Brilliant people learn from the experience of others throughout history.
- You can't do anything positive with a negative attitude. (38)

Index

About the Author
Richard V. Battle

Multi Award-Winning Author, Speaker, Media Personality and Advisor, Richard is the author of ten books focused on communicating messages promoting God and Country and personal growth enabling people to pursue their dreams and fulfill their life's journey.

He has been a public speaker and trainer for over 30 years on leadership, motivation, faith, sales, and volunteerism.

Richard was a corporate executive experienced in sales, executive management, and leadership in various business entities.

Texas Governor Rick Perry appointed him to The Texas Judicial Council and The Texas Emerging Technology Fund.

As president of the Austin Junior Chamber of Commerce, the U.S. Junior Chamber of Commerce recognized the chapter as the Most Outstanding chapter in the United States. The Junior Chamber of Commerce International recognized Richard as the Outstanding Chapter President in the world.

He served on the board of directors of Alpha Kappa Psi, an international professional business fraternity, and was a past chairman.

He has served on the board of many organizations, including Shepperd Leadership Institute (past chairman), Boy Scouts of America, Muscular Dystrophy Association, and Keep Austin Beautiful.

Richard is involved with the National Day of Prayer and has served as master of ceremonies for the Texas State Prayer Breakfast honoring the governor.

Richard lives in Lakeway, Texas. His mission is to communicate Positive messages helping people win every day!

Aim High!

Work Hard!

NEVER Quit! ®

Richard V. Battle Books

Made in America
By AmeriCANS not AmeriCANTS

Made In America by AmeriCANS not AmeriCANTS will inspire the reader and provide the tools to learn, lead, and leave a legacy benefitting those who follow us.

If you want to fulfill your dreams and destiny, this book's AmeriCAN principles and examples will accelerate your quest.

It includes 103 quotes, 108 Battle's Bullets, and 135 Sage Sayings.

Available in paperback, Kindle, Nook, and audio editions.

Life's Daily Treasure
366 Doses of Hope, Optimism,
Personal growth, and Encouragement

Does It Seem Like Hope Has Vanished?

You're Not Alone – Here are 366 Daily Doses.

Life's Daily Treasure is for adults seeking hope and encouragement in an ever-challenging world.

It is a book of hope for today and every day and an excellent gift for all occasions!

Its 2,196 entries of inspiration, motivation, and American celebration are wonderful resources for speakers, pastors, teachers, and others.

Available in Hardback, Paperback, and Kindle editions.

Navigating Life's Journey
Common Sense in Uncommon Times

If you liked *Conquering Life's Course*, you'll love this successor to it.

Forty bite-sized, easy-to-read chapters of time-proven principles will restore your confidence in your beliefs, encourage you to defend them, and inspire you to teach your sacred values to your loved ones. It will lift your spirits and restore your hope in America.

It includes 250 examples and 75 motivational quotes.

Available in paperback, Kindle, and audio editions.

Conquering Life's Course
Common Sense in Chaotic Times

Do you wonder if Common Sense is vanishing?

It will entertain and inspire the reader to think, laugh and undertake actions to realize a more fulfilling life.

If you or a loved one have given up on understanding the world of today, Conquering Life's Course is a must-read. It assures readers that age-old traditions and wisdom still rule over unproven theories.

It is concise, easy to read, and offers invaluable insights that readers can share with the entire family.

Available in paperback, Kindle, and audio editions.

Unwelcome Opportunity –
Overcoming Life's Greatest Challenges

What do you do when you experience divorce, two heart procedures, and a cancer diagnosis within ten months? It is the story of an ordinary man facing multiple life challenges in one ten-month period.

In it, you will see an example of God's presence and provision that helped Richard Battle traverse this turbulent period of his life.

Available in paperback, Kindle, Nook, and audio editions.

Surviving Grief by God's Grace

There is no greater loss in this world than losing one's child. This book is the first-person account of the author's loss of his first and then only child. It is a story of the grief, spiritual quest, and grace that helped Richard and his family survive and to live with hope for the future.

Available in paperback and Kindle editions.

The Four-Letter Word That Builds Character

Why are so many young people having a problem adapting to society today? Where have we gone wrong? Is it the parents or society in general? The Four-Letter Word That Builds Character can make a difference in this scattered and cluttered world. Based on the lessons learned from the author's first job and parental teaching of traditional values that have proven to be the foundation for lifelong success, this volume teaches 14 proven principles of a good work ethic and character.

Available in paperback Kindle and audio editions.

The Volunteer Handbook
How to Organize and Manage a Successful Organization

More than 75 topics provide specific ideas to help volunteer leaders maximize their efforts. Topics include Long-range, annual and event planning; Training board and prospective board members; how to recruit new members; ten steps to activate or reactivate a member; six steps to building a successful team; and How to motivate your membership. Effective Delegation. Managing non-performers.

Available in paperback

The Master's Sales Secrets
44 Strategies for Sensational Sales Success

Richard V. Battle offers business leaders a graduate-level class in what he learned over forty-plus years in sales and sales management. It is Practical, sharp, and clearly communicated. The Master's Sales Secrets can be read cover to cover or referenced strategy by strategy.

Available in paperback and Kindle editions.

***

"While I don't know where my path
will lead me, I know the destination.

If you have suggestions for future ideas, or would like additional clarification on my efforts, you can reach me at richard@richardbattle.com.

Thank you again for your support of my work,
and encouragement."